INTERNATIONAL WOMEN SPEAK

The Emergence of Women's Global Leadership

Women Speak Series No. 3

Introduction by Dr. Doris Earnshaw

Doris Earnshaw

ALTA VISTA PRESS
Davis, CA USA
2000

Published by

ALTA VISTA PRESS

P.O. Box 73675, Davis, CA 95617, USA

Tel/Fax: 530-756-1684; E-mail: avp@dcn.davis.ca.us

www.altavistapress.com

Women Speak Series No. 3

Cover design by Jeanne Pietrzak, Graphic Gold, Davis, CA

The speeches in this book are published by permission.

Library of Congress Control Number: 00-135826

ISBN: 0-9640574-1-7

Table of Contents

Dedicated to Children, especially

Tiago and Sofia Luxton
Lola and Eva Marrero
Jonnie Marie Ribera
Hatley Rose Evans Thompson

"The world is never ready
for the birth of a child. . ."*

---

*From the poem, "A Tale Begun" in *Wislawa Szymborska, view with a grain of sand selected poems* translated from the Polish by Stanislaw Baranczak and Clare Cavanagh, New York, Harcourt Brace & Company, 1995. Wislawa Szymborska was awarded the 1996 Nobel Prize for Literature.

Introduction

By presenting the ideas of women in public life, *International Women Speak* follows the form of the two previous "Women Speak" books, but it differs from them completely in its ambitious global reach. Volume 1: *California Women Speak*, was prepared in a familiar setting, with help from CEWAER, the California Elected Women's Association for Education and Research. The director, Dr. Kate Karpilow, was able to offer valuable advice, and wrote her introduction from her personal knowledge of each woman in the book.

Moving to the national level for Volume 2, *American Women Speak*, we also faced comparatively little difficulty, since each woman we invited to participate had a press secretary eager to supply several talks for us to choose from, and the press photograph and biography were sent from their ample supply. The unfortunate fact is, there were not many American women serving as Governors, Senators and Congresswomen to choose from, a situation which still has not altered significantly. Our approach was non-partisan; women across the political spectrum in local, state and national positions were included. Dr. Ruth Mandel, of Rutgers University's Eagleton Institute of Politics, graciously agreed to write her fine introduction.

Turning to the global political scene for Volume 3, we faced a different magnitude of choice and operational challenges, and were not so sure-footed. The book evolved slowly. In September, 1995, the Fourth United Nations World Conference on Women, the "Beijing Conference," provided plenty of inspiration. As a member of the press, I had all the privileges of access to a choice of events every hour. Somewhat like European medieval pilgrims returning from Santiago de Compostela, Rome or Jerusalem, we came back changed people, full of faith, confident of belonging to an unstoppable global movement.

Volume 3 first took shape with an emphasis on outstanding women from different countries. We looked for a Russian, a Chinese, a South African woman, and so on, to represent her nation. Soon the irrationality of a national approach for an international book became clear. The next approach was to develop a list of separate issues, one woman speaking for each: children, housing, war, peace, health, etc. The third and final shape arose from the women themselves – in the way they choose to serve the common good – as thinkers, administrators, advocates and players. From many countries, they are united by common goals: the necessity for a peaceful civil society, individual welfare in a healthy physical world, the importance of looking to the future, the legacy our children will inherit. And yet, many important areas of life are not represented here: science, the arts, religion. The contribution of women in those fields are fascinating and important. But the overarching protection of civil society seems to me to be a middle ground where a gender advance is critical. The genius leaders who will provide new energy to end the cycles of war and abuse, arouse our conscience about the environment, and make our world less fearful need governments where the counsel of women is respected and heard. Many women feel like the Spanish poet Gloria Fuertes, who says of herself in her poem, "Now"

> " . . . Because, though tiny, I know many things,
> and my body is an endless eye,
> through which, unfortunately, I see everything."

Two of the speeches here date from the earliest phase of the book's organization: Mary Robinson's talk which opens Part One, and Dr. Gro Harlem Brundtland's talk which opens Part Three. Both talks are from the mid-nineties, but to me seem dateless. The first combines historical and literary reflection with observations of women's groups as Robinson became the new President of Ireland. Dr. Brundtland also understands the full consequences of women's reproductive health care. Imagine the versatility of this medical doctor and President of Norway who stepped in to revive a passenger while flying to Beijing for the women's conference in 1995!

Not surprisingly, many of the speakers here are executives and administrators in the United Nations' programs around the world. The United Nations has set a world standard for gender balance in governing and deliberative bodies of 30-70%; i.e. any governing body should have no less than 30% and no more than 70% members of either gender. As Angela King reports, the UN Organization is meeting this goal. The UN web site with its news, speeches, reports and biographies demonstrates a commitment to effective communication. I thank the staff members of the UN and the support organization, UNA/USA, for their assistance.

Some of the speakers came to us from friends' recommendations; others from articles in the New York Times and similar news sources. During 1998, I had the unusual experience of "listening in" on global exchanges by email among women lawyers helping each other to find ways to activate "CEDAW" the United Nations Convention on the Elimination of Discrimination Against Women. It was new law many countries have agreed to, and the lawyers shared procedures for implementation. CEDAW, unfortunately, is almost unknown to the American public. The United States Senate has not even discussed, much less ratified it. But it was through that email exchange that I learned, among others, of Dianne Post, working in Russia on gender issues through cooperative arrangements of the Russian government and the American Bar Association.

We have included blank pages titled "Notes" to encourage readers to record their personal responses, questions and ideas. Readers will notice different spelling and punctuation which we have left according to the style in use by the people sending us text. We are setting up an interactive web site at www.altavistapress.com and hope to hear from many of you.

San Francisco area women have been wonderful organizers for women's issues. This book couldn't have happened without the inspiration and practical help of Marilyn Fowler, Judy Kramer, Helen Young and WIN, the Women's Intercultural Network. Women up and down the state work together in CAWA, the California Women's Agenda, "Bringing Beijing Home" with conferences and work groups. In June, 2000, they hosted a national conference of the National Association of Committees on the Status of Women. Yearly conferences at Mills College on women's leadership have also given important inspiration.

Dr. Nancy Zak shared her deep knowledge and passion about native North American people. Translation help came from my daughter, Linda Ribera for Spanish, Margaret Dutra for Portuguese, Anna Kaladiouk for Russian, Mayumi Saito of Davis for Japanese, as well as Jay Matsuda in the Osaka San Francisco Office. Joy Fergoda, Women's Resource Center librarian at the University of California at Davis sent international research material. Bill Blodgett was an early proofreader, and Shauna Scott, an intern, gave valuable and cheerful assistance. My Canadian cousin, Jean Grierson Smith, pitched in at critical moments, as did Denise B. Ribera and Marie Walker in New Zealand, Wendy Thompson, David Thompson. My daughter, Denise R. Luxton, made the final days fun. All three books in the series had the benefit of a nonpareil production team: Mary Doty and Jeanne Pietrzak. I thank each of them and so many others around the world who have responded eagerly to the project, sending it out into the world with their good will. And I owe an unspeakable debt to the twenty women featured here who show us the way to a healthy and less fearful future.

Doris Earnshaw
Davis, California

International Women Speak

Mary Robinson

*I*n only three years as the United Nations High Commissioner for Human Rights, Mary Robinson has become an articulate and highly visible opponent of human rights abuses. She often leaves the head office in Geneva to visit conflict areas where human rights staff members gather information to be used in prosecution of violators. In a recent radio interview,* she told of meeting child soldiers in a Sierra Leone shelter – children who had been drugged and forced into fighting and chopping off hands and feet of other children – they told her they just wanted to find their parents. When human rights workers are murdered, as happened recently in Indonesia, she feels as though she has lost family members. Such close encounters with tragedy and evil demand extraordinary emotional stamina.

Robinson feels well prepared for facing and negotiating conflict situations because her country, Ireland, has experienced the damages of colonialism, religious conflict and endemic violent confrontations. For twenty years she served in the Irish Senate, where she often stood against the majority opinion to advocate for women's rights to divorce law and birth control information. Because those protections were not then legal in her home territory, she took her cases to the European Union courts.

Always highly respected for her personal integrity and judicial temperament, she was elected President of Ireland in 1991 and served seven years in that office. A Catholic, she will soon celebrate thirty years of marriage – to a Northern Irish Protestant – a personal example of her genius to see beyond divisions to harmony.

<u>Editor's Note</u>: I have loved this talk since Mary Robinson sent it to me some years ago. In a beautiful writing style, she calls for "deep and generous shifts in our established thinking." She argues for gender balance in public life on three persuasive grounds: first, the emotional damage done to women from being treated like a child; second, the value of women's <u>inclusive style</u> of group organization, in which "individuality is safe" and third, the benefit to both men and women of "listening to the other" in an attitude of appreciation for the different political styles of men and women. She sets the stage for the rest of the book, in which women's voices unfold their achievements, hopes, concerns and demands.

---

*National Public Radio interview September, 2000 with Terry Gross, Fresh Air, WHYY Philadelphia, PA, USA.

Mary Robinson

United Nations High Commissioner for Human Rights
Republic of Ireland

Mary Robinson

[From the Allen Lane Foundation Memorial Lecture given at Trinity College, Dublin, February 25, 1992. Mary Robinson had recently been elected President of Ireland.]

"STRIKING A BALANCE"

When I selected this title for tonight's lecture I was acutely aware that to many people the term striking a balance might suggest an evasive or overly-tactful approach to the issue of women's role and rights. I want to emphasise here at the start that the balance I would like to see struck is not an awkward coming-to-terms or a last minute compromise. Far from it. It must be a comprehensive re-assessment of the place and contribution of a woman in her society.

If the imbalances of the past came, as I believe they did, not simply from legislative injustices and economic inequality but from profound resistances and failures of perception, then it follows that to right that balance we must do more than review our legislation and re-state our economic structures. We must also fundamentally re-appraise our view of who and what is valuable in our society. We must look with fresh and unprejudiced eyes at the work of women, the views of women, their way of organising and their interpretation of social priorities. To achieve this, we must, I believe, begin at the beginning and alter our way of thinking.

It will be one of my arguments tonight that at the moment equality between the sexes is seen to be a women's issue. It is not. It is said to be a marginal issue. It is not. It is perceived as a threat to the traditional structures of a society. And it is not. But because of these flawed interpretations the approach to achieving equality has been similarly flawed. It remains an ad hoc approach. We make legislative changes and appoint women in response to organised insistence and the pressure of public opinion. Therefore the accounting of progress is recorded less through deep and generous shifts in established thinking, and more by listing laws or doing a number count of the women in public positions. This ad hoc approach ensures that the issue of women's equality is starved of reflective thinking and careful planning. It is, of course, important that women participate more in all sectors of modern societies, but it is not sufficient. The elusive balance requires a more fundamental re-evaluation of the role, the worth and the contribution of all women in their society.

I propose tonight that if we are to strike a balance we will have to reflect. We will have to look closely and carefully at what is there now and how it can accommodate new energies and real creative forces which still remain outside the power structures of the established order. Such a balance needs to be struck. It will require careful thought and a listening posture. It will also require a clearminded analysis of how we absorb the creativity of women into our society and where we fail to do so. Only by listening and thoughtful analysis can we come up with the answers to these questions. I don't suggest to you here tonight that I have all the answers. But it has been one of the privileges of my first year as President of Ireland that I have been able to witness and to listen. I want to bring you the result of that tonight and to cast it in the form of an analysis of these energies and how we interpret them.

Let me begin with a backward glance. The last hundred years – I think we are all aware of this – have seen great shifts in the area of women's equality. During this period, in the West, in democratic societies, the rights of women came under scrutiny as never before. I think it is important that we don't grow complacent about this. We need to remember and celebrate – and never take for granted – the courage and persistence of those who brought about shifts of perception and legislation. They have changed our world. The past was a darker place for women than we like to remember. Yet we need to remember. Even the most cursory glance at it will show how far we have come and how necessary the journey was.

George Eliot once wrote "The happiest women, like the happiest nations, have no history". In Ireland, where we have a powerful history, we can provide a gloss to her statement. But whether you agree with her or not, I think we know that the recorded history of women is poignantly incomplete. My first backward glance, which suggests both the absence of the record, and therefore a corrective to that absence, is Virginia Woolf's comment in her essay "Women and Fiction".

"Very little is known about women", she writes. *"The history of England is the history of the male line, not of the female. Of our fathers we know always some fact, some distinction. They were soldiers or they were sailors; they filled that office or they made that law. But of our mothers, our grandmothers, our great-grandmothers, what remains? Nothing but a tradition. One was beautiful; one was red-haired. One was kissed by a queen. We know nothing of them except their names and the dates of their marriages and the number of children they bore".*

Virginia Woolf 's statement suggests both the strength and frustration of unrecorded history. Now, in the second backward glance, I want to quote a remarkable Chinese woman called Qiu Jin who lived at the end of the last century. She was a poet and a journalist. She founded the Chinese Women's Journal. In this extract from one of her essays she addresses the subject of education:

"My beloved sisters: though I am not a person of great scholarly attainments, I am someone who loves her country and her compatriots with all her heart. And isn't it true that we number four hundred million? But the two hundred million who are men have gradually begun to take part in the enlightenment of the modern age: their knowledge has increased, their outlook has broadened, their level of scholarship has risen and their reputation is advancing day by day. This is all due to the fact that they have access to books and periodicals. Isn't theirs an enviable position? But, alas, while these two hundred million men and boys have entered the enlightened new age, my two hundred million countrywomen are still mired in the darkness of the eighteen levels of their earthly prison,

with no thought of advancing even a single stage. Their feet are bound small, their hair is dressed to a shine; they wore ornaments of buds and blossoms, carved and inlaid; on their bodies are silk and satin, rippling and shimmering. Their whole lives long they learn nothing but how to comply".

This is a bleak and persuasive challenge which Qiu Jin puts before her countrywomen. Yet, in some sense, we recognise in it the tones of hope. It is, at least, forceful. Qiu Jin is able to give shape to her criticism. But I am deliberately, in these examples, moving back in time and sketching the picture in darker tones as I go. So let me darken that picture again with a quotation from the book "Incidents in the Life of a Slave Girl" by Harriet A. Jacobs. Describing New Year's Day – which under the writ of slavery was auction day – she says:

"On one of those days I saw a mother lead seven children to the auction block. She knew that some of them would be taken from her but they took all. The children were sold to a slave trader and their mother was bought by a man in her own town. Before night her children were all far away. She begged the trader to tell her where he intended to take them: this he refused to do. How could he, when he knew he would sell them one by one, for the highest price. I met that mother in the street and her wild, haggard face lives today in my mind."

These three instances of challenge and suffering reach back through more than a hundred years of change and the necessity for change. It seems to me that they have one thing in common. Though the levels of distress in them are certainly different – the quiet continuity which Virginia Woolf finds a deprivation Harriet Jacobs would have felt to be a luxury – yet they do share a vital element. They are all the accounts of articulate women. They are the claims of articulate women and made in the interests of those with no voice. The self-definition and eloquence in each of them reminds us, if we need to be reminded, that articulateness – often on behalf of and in place of the voiceless – is an essential part of women's equality. It is part and parcel of the presentation I make to you tonight.

All this comes near the heart of my argument. We cannot strike a balance until we right the imbalances which already exist. In the area of women's equality this has meant, and still means, re-arranging the order of participation and the access to self-expression, so that men and women have an equal chance to make their contribution and find their creativity in a society which *neither* owns and *both* share. But how are we to achieve this?

I began by saying that I am neither a scientist nor sociologist. And so the view I put forward now is very much based on my own experience. It is the outcome, partly of my background in law and in my family, and very much of this last year when I have been a privileged witness and observer. It is also necessarily limited to the experience of Western democratic societies, although I have had valuable insights into the extraordinarily creative role of women in developing countries, which – notwithstanding that that role differs in priorities and emphasis – has reinforced my overall view.

Having made that careful disclaimer, I want to venture the idea that some of the ways in which women articulate their sense of a society and of the priorities within it seems to me to be very creative, very worth listening to, and often entirely different from the structures which are already in place. During this past year, so many of the women I have met are obviously articulate. The way they organise is, strikingly, an outcome of it. But it is more than that. Their ability to devise structures, to order priorities, to assemble an agenda and construe a commitment is not only eloquent. To me it often looks distinctive and creative and therefore a style of problem-solving which is different from the ones we are used to in the public and visible power centres of our society.

And yet I am not sure their vision *is* reaching the places in our society where such power is established. I am not sure these eloquent, original statements are being heard. The reason for this may well be that they are different. The visible and established ways of doing things – the law courts, the councils, the academies, the board rooms – are often respectful of tradition and governed by precedent. The structures I am thinking of – and which I have seen women proposing over and over again this past year – are original and often radical. They are not so much dismissive of precedent as unable to afford the delay involved in considering it.

I have come to believe these structures are different because they originate in a different set of perceptions. If we wanted to be historical, we could argue that they come from that silence Virginia Woolf described. Or they may have been excluded from the education Qiu Jin longed for. They may even remember the injustices Harriet Jacobs records. But aren't they all the more valuable for that? Don't they have a great deal to offer the structures which are already in place? I am not suggesting that one replace the other. I am not suggesting that one obstruct the other. I am arguing that they may have something to learn from each other, and they cannot do so unless they listen to each other.

I have tried to outline the idea of structures in a society listening to one another, carrying on a sort of dialogue which might modify both. This may seem far fetched. In fact, if we look at the area of women's rights, this has been happening for a long time in a sort of hand to mouth, unconscious way. Let me take one example. The whole cause of equality for women has often had to go forward as a protest movement. At different times there have been rallies, pamphlets, meetings, test cases in the courts. Today we see this movement in perspective, and we acknowledge our debt to it. We know it was often carried forward by isolated women under difficult circumstances and with triumphant effect.

But if we look close for a moment we can see that the means of that advance – the printing press, the vote, the right to organise, the test case – these are all methods and modes of protest and progress devised by men of conscience, set up within oppressive power structures and often won at great cost. The plain truth is that, in the definition of women's rights, the freedoms gained by men have played an important part. So here we have one structure speaking to another – a sort of dialogue which is both redemptive and effective. Is it utopian to argue that what has happened in an improvisational way – in the rush and instinct of protest – could continue in a rational and fruitful way in our day-to-day lives?

And yet, despite the need for such a dialogue, it is still incomplete. Many of us are aware that the creative energies of women are still very imperfectly absorbed into modern societies.

Such energies are still thought of as appropriate to women's concerns – which of course they are. But they are less often thought of as crucial to the whole society. And yet they are.

If we don't have the answers to this anomaly then the next best thing is to pose the questions. We have – in women, in their organisational abilities, in their creative approach – a major resource. It is not being fully used. And yet we know that there have been extensive changes and real progress. So in time of legislative reform and visible advance it seems both inconsistent and disappointing to be talking about a fracture between one structure and another, a lack of communication between one group and another. But as I said at the start, striking a balance requires generosity and fresh perspective rather than logic or programmatic thinking.

We have to accept that resistances and missed opportunities frequently do not happen at visible levels. Every society maintains an invisible life where attitudes and assumptions are formed. Every society is hostage to this unseen place, where fear conquers reason and old attitudes remain entrenched. It is here that the chance phrases and small asides are made which say so little and reveal so much. If we are to go forward we need to look at attitudes and the language which expresses attitude. And all of this can be locked into very small details. I think we are aware that very often if something – whether a book or a social issue or an occasion – is said to be for women, there is often an inference, even today, that it is only for women. And from there it is a short step to suggesting that it is merely for women. If we are to strike a balance, if we are to re-adjust participation and enrich our society with dialogue, we have to revise this way of thinking.

All of this has been very much at the front of my mind in the past year. I have witnessed these energies for myself. I have seen these energies in community and information centres, counselling, educational and care groups, creative workshops and artists' collectives. I don't want to make a false or over-inclusive assessment of different achievements. But many of these occasions and many of these projects seem to me to have been put together with the distinctive organisational skills I have mentioned. I could talk about very small details which remain in my mind. After all, I was trained in the law, one of the oldest of the organisational sciences. It is based on precedent, and one spokesperson interprets the issues on behalf of many. I think that is a way in which many of the established organs of our society work.

From that background, it was fascinating for me to observe – even in a preliminary and unscientific way – a different style of doing things. Often everyone in the group spoke to me. Everyone was encouraged to have their say. There was an alternative running order. I am not saying this sort of detail represents a hard and fast difference between women's groups or community gatherings and the rest of society. But I do suggest that there are fresh, improvisational responses in these groups to the contemporary challenges of our society.

Earlier this month I met with groups of women in Belfast. They spoke to me about the concerns of their local areas, the common problems and interests, the projects which are going forward, their deep commitment to family and community. They came from all parts of Belfast, from Derry and from right across rural Northern Ireland. I was fascinated and moved by their conversation, their energy, their story-telling, their humour and their warmth. And one thing struck me with great force. In such groups, it seems to me, <u>individuality is safe</u>. There is a great relish for the distinctive person, the difference of method, the divergence of opinion. A profound sense of the richness of diversity, and its importance, came from their discussions and their respect for each other. Their presence and courage are an enormous resource to their society.

There are real rewards in looking afresh at the way we balance the contribution of women and the historical structures already in place. Where women have moved from small groups to collective effort, I think it has been strikingly for the good. A practical illustration is the whole area of voluntary effort. Women have shaped the voluntary effort worldwide. Their contribution has a fresh, problem-solving look to it. It by-passes bureaucracies and fills in the crevices between the rhetoric of help and the reality of providing it. Any study of the voluntary sector in modern society shows the same spirit at work. Just as women have infused the voluntary sector, so they can infuse and enrich the established structures of society.

In the past year I have used one of Yeats's phrases so often that if his estate were not out of copyright I might be accused of having infringed it! It's that beautiful remark he makes when he is talking of building a national theatre. He speaks of "a community bound together by imaginative possessions". In Ireland we know how strong that bond can be. In a dark moment, in an otherwise luminous text, Peig Sayers writes:

"Those whom I had known in my youth ... they all fell, they were all cleared out of the world. Those who had been there before them had met the same fate. God help us, where are their works today? Others are in their places without the least remembrance of them".

Her words remind us of the task of remembrance and the need to count and conserve our imaginative possessions. And in this community they are many. We have a powerful culture, a literature which celebrates it, a balance between tradition and the contemporary which many nations would give a great deal to have.

If we are to conserve our possessions, if we are to use our resources, we need to give some time and thought to an imaginative re-structuring. I believe we need an imaginative re-assessment of our attitudes and needs as a community so that we can bring to the centre those energies which are still just at the margin. Once and for all we need to commit ourselves to the concept that women's rights are not factional or sectional privileges, bestowed on the few at the whim of the few. They are human rights.

In a society in which the rights and potential of women are constrained, no man can be truly free. He may have power but he will not have freedom. Above all, if we continue to interpret the rights of women as the rights of women only, then we will miss the opportunity to draw into our society those powerful, enriching energies which it so needs.

At my inauguration as President of Ireland, I said:

"As a woman, I want women who have felt themselves outside history to be written back into history, in the words of Eavan Boland, 'finding a voice where they found a vision'."

Tatiana Dmitrieva

Dianne Post, an American lawyer who worked in Russia with the ABA-CEELI, [American Bar Association-Central and East European Law Initiative] sent this portrait:

"Tatiana Dmitrieva is the regional and international programs coordinator for the Tomsk regional government. She worked for two years as an aide in the national legislature and specializes in lobbying. She is an ardent supporter of quotas for women in political parties, and I saw her persuade a large group of women to her position at a conference in St. Petersburg in April, 1999.

She was the driving force behind an organizing campaign to open a mammography center in Tomsk. Their successful outreach resulted in contributions, 10 rubles, 1 ruble and even 10 kopeks, in battered brown envelopes trickling in from the farthest corners of the region. Working with ABA CEELI, she has trained women all over Russia how to lobby and organize using her mammography center as a practical example. Tall, blonde and athletic, with a strong singing voice, Tanya has a daughter in her 20's and a *dacha* [summer cottage] with the most fabulous vegetable garden tended by her father."

Editor's note: Many women recognize the heartfelt sense of injustice that Dmitrieva expresses so eloquently. One sentence captures the feeling, "He must have as many women as men in his constituency, but he fails to attend to their particular interests ..." The "particular interests," clearly expressed in the 1995 Beijing Declaration, will become visible as legislatures become gender balanced.

Placing quotas for women on election slates has become a live issue in many countries. It has an interesting history in Taiwan. After the second world war, a quota of 5% women in the legislature was instituted by Mme. Chiang Kai-shek, wife of the political ruler. She reasoned that since about 5% of women in Taiwan were educated, the increase from zero to 5% would advance women in politics. That early quota became a "limit" and had to be fought later on, as Taiwan established a more democratic government. The newly elected (spring, 2000) vice-president of Taiwan, Annette Lu, was part of the "anti-quota" effort.

Tatiana Dmitrieva

Regional and International Programs Coordinator,
Tomsk Regional Government
Russia

Tatiana Dmitrieva

[Written by request for *International Women Speak*]

"WHY DID I BECOME A FEMINIST?"

*T*o begin, I would like to refer you to Joyce Stevens, British feminist, who claims "women's work is never done, unpaid or less paid, or dull and routine, we are the first to be fired and our looks matter more than what we do; if we are raped, that is our fault, if we are beaten; it is we who provoked it; if we raise our voice, we are row-makers; if we enjoy sex, we are nymphomaniacs, and if not, we are frigid; and when we expect society to care about children we are egoistic; if we stand for our rights, we are aggressive and unfeminine, and if we do not, then we are typical weak women; if we want to get married, we are husband hunters, and if we do not, we are not normal." These and many other reasons make us participate in the women's movement.

I have been working side by side with men for almost ten years. Anyway, one who does not work among women, works in a predominantly male environment.

I entered politics some time ago from being "a modest teacher." That was how one prominent Tomsk man liked to describe me. Now he holds a powerful position in Moscow. My coming to politics happened in the time of changes. At the dawn of democratic changes, I worked with men exclusively. Women were there to help men – men who were all-knowing and omnipotent. Men were the vehicles of new ideology. They initiated the change. However, that time liberated women, but the fruits of that time can be seen only today. I grew politically among men, gaining experience and learning a lot. I noticed that men appreciated my serving them, not my participation in politics. Once I saw that a big party delegation included a woman only as a gesture of conciliation.

My feminism might have started when a leader of the present city administration saw me tidying up the room, and said, "Finally the woman is doing her work." I was cleaning the headquarters of "restructuring revolution" ("perestroika") where political administrators came to direct the first steps of democratic reform, as I then naively believed. Later I realized that from there they were unleashing a struggle for power and the benefits it confers. When I got to the State Duma (parliament), I saw that Ykaterina Lakhova was making men sick with her activity and zest, while the votes of her "Women of Russia" faction dissatisfied the communist and democratic wings equally. All parties wanted to have the women's vote. A Deputy I had been working for commented on a woman member of the Duma, "...a beautiful woman, but I would rather she kept silent." Every time a woman speaks publicly, men react emotionally, not rationally.

I first met a great number of active women in 1993 when I took part in a big international women's conference in Veliki Novgorod. There I met plenty of intelligent, well-educated and dedicated women. They were looking forward to changes and believed in them. We had numerous seminars, meetings with women who were famous, known all over the country. I came to see this as a great power. As early as 1993, self-aware Russian women soared to such heights, and this led to creation of the election block, "Women of Russia" which won a place in the parliamentary election.

So why does this question of women persist? What is the quest for a social role and a place for women?

Feminism in Russia is not popular. A woman who calls herself a feminist runs the risk of losing a man's affection. The consequences are even graver in the city of Tomsk. Feminism is more popular in the capital, Moscow, and in the big cities of the European part of Russia. Further away, beyond the Urals, there is less information about it, and it produces greater dislike. Even though most Russians have very little idea of feminism, the little they have is likely to be distorted. Any kind of free thinking in women is unwelcome. But a dictionary of foreign words defines "feminism" as "a women's movement of equal rights with men, for an increased role and influence of women in society." Nothing to be afraid of.

Let me put everyone at ease: feminism in Russia did not acquire repulsive forms as it has sometimes in the West. Our feminists wash our hair, have it done, cut our nails and have manicures, use make-up, and do not cut off men's organs throwing them away onto the road. On the whole, feminists are educated, intelligent and reserved people. The peculiarity of Russian feminism is that it has not reached the grassroots; it has not won over young people and men. Russian feminism manifests itself in women's efforts to assert their rights to see life in their own way. It manifests itself in their free thinking.

Mass culture, that turns a woman into a consumption object, the cult of consumption being imposed on her, gave an impetus to wider dissemination of ideas of feminism. It made people voice their protest against consuming attitudes toward women. Of course, making a choice between the cult of consumerism and dignity, naturally most Russians, including women, have chosen consumerism. Women associated with the women's movement and those standing for interests of their friends, hurry to distance themselves from feminism. Our society is organized according to how men imagine it and think about it, for their own sake. In a society where women think mostly about pleasing men, feminism does not enjoy much respect. Even though our local press does not say much about the movement and our central press does not spend too much time discussing it either; even though we don't have many examples of militant women who fight for men's annihilation or simply preach the rights and interests of women, people still don't like feminism.

I think men should not be concerned that feminism might get out of hand. In Russia, a woman is too dependent on a man, both economically and psychologically. She is oriented toward traditional values too much. She is too busy either trying to survive, or to consume.

I do not think we should force the dissemination of feminism or that women should stand in rows under a banner. Still, what sorts of problems make us think of singing out about the woman question? We should be thinking about the problems that specifically affect women:

Unemployment Women's incomes are falling dramatically, and feminized poverty is soaring. Women make up 70% of the unemployed in Russia, and in the Tomsk region, up to 60% are jobless.

Age Discrimination This is not a new problem, but it has become acute. It is no secret that the majority of classified ads listing employment set an applicant age limit of 35, sometimes even 25, and some applicants must be "European looking" or "attractive." Employers do not recruit women who have small children. In the United States, a question about children in a job interview could be considered discrimination, and the woman could take the case to court. In Russia, nobody even tries to impose sanctions on companies for this practice. Here, in Russia, there is a common understanding that no law can be imposed on private enterprise.

Payments for Child Welfare For some reason, this is considered purely a women's problem. Traditionally, in our society, women are the ones who care for children, although the whole family suffers when the payment is not made.

Arrears in State Institutions' Salaries This problem affects women more than men in our city and region because most minor state employees are women.

Domestic Violence and Sexual Harassment at Work These problems have not yet been realized by wide sections of Russian women, but they do exist. I keep a Tomsk newspaper ad that reads: "Beauties. Round the Clock. Jobs for girls. Housing provided." I remember a call from a woman pleading for help because of sexual violence at home.

I sometimes ask myself whether it is proper to raise issues like these when people face the problem of finding food to eat. However, we must write about them. A permanent orientation to self-limitation and self-victimization is a sign of an unhealthy society.

In addition, the problem of participation of women in power structures is not the least of women's problems. It is generally accepted that nothing and nobody prevents a woman from making a career in politics or power institutions. Then, I ask, why do women account for only 7% in the State Duma? Why only one woman out of 178 members of the Federation Council (and we hardly ever see her on TV screens)? Why are there only two women among all the ministers? Why are there only 3 women out of 42 deputies in the Tomsk Region Duma, and only 3 in the Regional Administration?

And why are there no women to be found among leaders of the political parties?

No answer is given. I once suggested to the editor of a Tomsk newspaper to raise the problem in his paper. His answer was that there is no such topic. It does not interest him. But if I could give him some concrete names of people who prevent women from coming to power, then it might be interesting as a problem. Besides being a blind and narrow-minded journalist, the man is a deputy to one of the legislative bodies of our region. He must have as many women as men in his constituency, yet he fails to attend to their particular interests because it is not proper in our society to divide the world into men's and women's spheres. It is one world: men's.

For myself, I would like to ask: is there any room for feminism in the Tomsk region?

If a woman wishes to work actively to develop society, to improve it or simply to protect her rights and dignity, and if that wish requires her to work in power structures, and at the same time she doesn't want to be an object of scorn, should she be blamed?

Bronagh Hinds

Founder and negotiator for the Women's Coalition of Northern Ireland, Bronagh Hinds promoted women's peace demands and women's right to organize and lobby for political aims. She helped to build the Coalition on years of women's activism – activism that needed a channel to develop and grow. In the face of scoffing admonitions from legislators to "quit whining" and "to go home and breed," she brought women to the forefront on such key policy issues as human rights, peace and equality.

Her opponents were dealing with a woman whose leadership gifts were evident from her student days when she was president of the student union at Queen's University of Belfast. From 1975 to 1990, she organized and led a range of volunteer groups: in pre-school education for children, anti-poverty programs and consumer education. She served as area director for Oxfam in Ireland in 1990, until in 1992 she became the Director of Ulster People's College, a position she presently holds.

In the wider European scene, she has been Chair of numerous commissions, including the Northern Ireland Women's European Platform, the Joint Committee of the European Women's Lobby, and the Northern Ireland UN Beijing Working Group. She is the Founding Secretary of the European Anti-Poverty Network.

In 1999, she was selected United Kingdom Woman of Europe – a prestigious award that recognizes women's efforts in the political community. Many publications and research papers reflect her interests. She is a popular speaker at home and abroad on topics of policy development at local, national and international levels.

In her spare time, Hinds enjoys browsing art exhibits, folk dancing, swimming and, never one to keep hobbies and work too far apart, discussing national and international politics.

Editor's note: Moved into action by the deaths of three young children in a skirmish between IRA and British soldiers, Protestant Betty Williams, who witnessed the tragedy, and Catholic Mairead Corrigan, the children's aunt, organized weekly marches of "Peace People" in Belfast to protest religious violence. In spite of being called "traitors" and death threats, they brought people together who had been "enemies." They won the Nobel Peace Prize of 1977.

Bronagh Hinds

Deputy High Commissioner, Equality Commission for
Northern Ireland, Director, Ulster People's College
Northern Ireland

Bronagh Hinds

[Excerpts from Address to the Beijing + 5 Preparatory Conference, San Francisco, California, February, 2000]

"MOVING THE AGENDA GLOBALLY"

*I*n the invitation to address this conference, I was asked to speak about the Northern Ireland Women's Coalition from my experience as a founder and campaign manager in our successful bid to be elected to the Peace Talks. I have also been the Coalition's negotiations co--ordinator for the two years of formal talks between Northern Ireland and the Republic of Ireland.

The Northern Ireland Women's Coalition was built upon years of women's activism, especially at the grassroots community level. As noted in the Northern Ireland NGO Report to Beijing, women have successfully worked to develop their own communities; they have campaigned on issues of equality, rights and justice and led peace movements springing from a concern for and affinity with victims of violence. As Melanne Verveer said, women have created a space for dialogue and successfully networked across the religious and political divide.

Nevertheless, the Women's Coalition was not something that had been planned, or even envisaged as the next and inevitable step in the Women's Movement; even by those most active and intimately involved in its establishment. When I spoke on International Women's Day in Cork in March, 1996, about the exclusion of women from politics, I had no concept that a few short weeks later, I, with others, would be founding a political party. Having failed to get existing parties to give consideration to equality-proofing their candidate selections, the Northern Ireland Women's European Platform successfully lobbied Government for an extension of the election legislation to include more parties so as to ensure greater access for women.

The Women's Coalition arose suddenly because its moment in time had arrived. With the certain knowledge that women would be left out of negotiating the future basis of our society, we realized that no effective option existed other than the Women's Coalition. We also had begun to appreciate that the absence of women was having a negative impact on the peace process. To put it bluntly, if women were involved, we would do it differently. Women's anger at the situation turned into determination to do something about it.

Once the decision was made, women swung into organisation. The Coalition drew women in from everywhere; women who were already active and women who were motivated by a desire for change. Women from all sides, classes and sectors. To deviate for a moment, I would like to stress the importance of education to democracy and participation. It was often said that the

Women's Coalition was middle-class, but research on Coalition candidates in the election showed that the Coalition comprised working class women too. The interesting thing was that many of these women shared a common factor – they had been adult returners to education.

The Women's Coalition was new and refreshing in its concept and approach. It credited the experience and skills which women brought, targeted those in community activity. It gave women the belief that they had the ability to stand for election. All candidates for the Women's Coalition signed a statement of values, comprising a commitment to inclusion, equity, human rights, diversity, and willingness to work for a political accommodation.

Seventy women contested the election for the Women's Coalition seven weeks after its inception. It was the fifth largest party in the election. Two women were elected on the basis of a regional list under the new electoral system.

How were such a large number of women candidates achieved for the first time and how was it done so quickly? A mixture of encouragement and press-ganging. Engaging women through existing activism and networks. Placing stories and advertisements asking women to put themselves forward. Handholding and running training workshops; providing resource materials and easily understood policy statements; brain storming and knowledge pooling; raising and sharing human and financial resources and providing backup such as childcare for meetings. This was all done in frenzy and in seven weeks. It was also fun – and possibly the best action learning programme on politics for women to date.

The Women's Coalition brought a will to succeed, and a determination to interrupt the culture of failure which had dogged Northern Ireland for decades. It brought a solid track record in new forms of thinking, problem solving and working for solution. It brought a history of confronting and respecting difference, as well as a record of transcending difference in pursuit of a common purpose. Unlike other parties, the Coalition was "process" orientated as well as "outcome" focused. It brought an agenda enlightened by three principles: inclusion, human rights, and equality. It applied these throughout the negotiations and ensured they were reflected in the language and the thrust of the Peace Agreement.

The Northern Ireland Peace Agreement is a more extensive agreement establishing the grounds for a political settlement than many other similar treaties. It covers more than new constitutional arrangements and the normal security and criminal justice issues surrounding a conflict. As well as giving input to these matters, the Women's Coalition successfully argued for references to equality and human rights, to victims as well as prisoners, to community development and to women's full and equal participation in political and public life. While the Coalition lost its argument for an electoral mechanism which would assist in putting greater numbers of women into politics, it succeeded in having its number one priority of a Civic Forum included. The Coalition believes that in any society, but most keenly in a society moving out of conflict, responsibility for the future must be shared more widely, more sectors of society must be involved in policy formulation and working relationships between politicians and those from business, trade union and community interests must be developed and enhanced.

But it is too easy to look back and register only the success. There was considerable pain as well as pleasure in the progress. The Coalition set out to transform and radicalise democracy, to challenge old behaviour and attitudes and set new standards of respect and competence. In Northern Ireland, as in many societies in conflict, an abnormal and deviant political culture existed. This took the form of a language and behaviour which set out to vilify and demonise, and which was a barrier not just to political progress but to opening up politics to greater participation, and thus change. Quite simply, people were turned off.

The political parties from a paramilitary background which were fully committed to pursuing a political accommodation bore the brunt of this. But the Women's Coalition also came in for its fair share of sectarianism, sexism and downright misogyny. Some anti-agreement elements on the Unionist side referred to 'whinging' 'whining' and 'feckless' women; called some of the Coalition's members 'traitors' – life threatening insult in Northern Ireland; "mooed" at the Coalition as if women were cows; and admonished women to go home and "breed for Ulster". Many male politicians were just not used to women in politics, and certainly not to women who did not toe the line! In the words of one "the Ulster woman in the past has seen herself very much in support of her man". The Coalition's response was a round of that well known country and western song "Stand by your man"!

However, progress since signing the Peace Agreement has been slow and difficult. As you know we are now in great danger of forfeiting the best chance we have ever had for our future based on a very comprehensive agreement. It is no surprise that this lack of momentum coincides with the fact that negotiation on the Agreement's implementation has narrowed both in agenda and participation. The ten parties formerly involved were reduced to just two or three for the main dialogue. The inclusive approach adopted for the negotiations has been discarded to our cost. Women, too, have once again been excluded from the main dialogue. However, even in the midst of our current difficulties, I have no reason to believe that we will not succeed. There is a deep-seated wish for settlement among civic leaders and people generally which our politicians cannot ignore.

What are the key lessons from the Northern Ireland peace process? And what difference, what unique contribution, can women make to the political process?

First, women can promote new forms of governance built on democratic values of equality, participation, accountability and transparency. Second, as women who have experienced the frustration of exclusion from power and its effect on our lives, we can uphold the principle of inclusivity. Third, we can recognise and enhance the role of grassroots community development in engaging and expressing active citizenship. The Northern Ireland experience demonstrates the importance of community development in securing women's involvement and in building an access route into formal politics.

We should not underestimate the importance of international support during times of great conflict in a country. We have received considerable support in Northern Ireland from the United States and the European Union for which we are very grateful. The Clinton administration has invested more time in Northern Ireland than any previous United States administration, and this has been important and welcome. Not only have we had the benefit of Senator George Mitchell's experience over many years, but President Clinton has visited twice and Mrs. Clinton has come no less than three times. In 1998, Mrs. Clinton attended a Vital Voices conference in Belfast, and since that conference there have been exchanges and networks on, for example, women in political life, and on childcare and family-friendly working. I also remember speaking at the final plenary of the ECE preparatory conference for Beijing held in Vienna in 1994, following the announcement of the first IRA ceasefire. As we moved towards a period of political dialogue, it was important for us to be able to make links with and to draw support from other women present in Vienna and from the strategies being pursued in the UN Platform for Action.

We need to make women visible in peace-making at all levels, including the political level. The United States, just like the European Union, is a significant player in interventions in conflicts and wars. I appreciate that Secretary of State Madelaine Albright has a key role, but nevertheless interventions from both the United States and the European Union are overwhelmingly male; they also most often play to a single track agenda, usually territory, political carve up and security.

Our experience in Northern Ireland shows that we need to change the dynamic within conflicts. The task of peace building must be more inclusive, opening out to enable and encourage local communities and various interests to participate and share responsibility for the future. We should engage in multi-track diplomacy, by supporting those active in civic leadership and at grassroots level in their peace endeavours and by encouraging their interaction and engagement with political negotiators and vice versa. As women are most often found at these secondary levels, this is an important aspect of empowering women in situations of conflict, and one which can also have a dramatic impact on securing the kind of inclusive settlement which is most likely to lead to sustainable success and stability.

In the United States and the European Union, we are keen on talking about the access of women to decision-making in our own countries, but what are we doing about it in solidarity with women who find themselves in difficult circumstances where our governments undoubtedly have influence? We must ask the United States and the European Union to include women prominently in their intervention delegations in order to "role model" that political democracy means that women as well as men must be at the negotiating table. In addition, those women who are on delegations should seek out and engage in dialogue with women locally and nationally within the country in conflict, to demonstrate the interdependency of the negotiating table and civic society, and to ease the access of women to positions of political influence. This is an international action in support of women in situations of conflict that can be worked on effectively.

Thank you for giving me the opportunity to be here with you.

Louise Fréchette

$\mathcal{L}$ouise Fréchette symbolizes the ideal of political cooperation within her bi-cultural nation and in her international leadership. Born in Montreal, Canada, July 16, 1946, Louise Fréchette is a graduate of Collège Basile Moreau. She earned degrees from the University of Montreal, and a post-graduate diploma in economic studies from the College of Europe at Bruges, Belgium, in 1978. She was awarded an Honorary Doctorate of Laws from Saint Mary's University in Halifax.

Fréchette began her political career in 1971, joining the Western European Division of Canada's Department of External Affairs, going to New York in her country's delegation to the United Nations in 1972. She then went on to Athens, Greece, as Second Secretary at the Canadian Embassy, 1973-75.

Her diplomatic and executive skills were soon recognized, and at 30, she represented Canada as First Secretary at the Permanent Mission to the United Nations in Geneva, Switzerland. She became Canada's Ambassador to Argentina, with responsibilities also in Uruguay and Paraguay. Within the Department, she served in several high-ranking positions. Having realized the potential and importance of international friendships, Fréchette worked to streamline Canada's relations with other countries, and was director of a review of Canada's relations with Latin American countries.

In 1992, she was Canada's Ambassador to the United Nations in New York. She was called back later to serve in Ottawa as an executive in the Departments of Finance and National Defense. Since February, 1998, she has held the newly established office of Deputy Secretary of the United Nations, placing her second in rank to Secretary General Kofi Annan.

Editor's Note: Today women hold leadership positions in global organizations such as the Soroptimists, the Rotary Club, Amnesty International, International Women's Business Organization, Global Exchange, and Sister Cities. Fréchette's career began in international diplomacy, an area then as now less open to women. Her outstanding success is a tribute to her gifts and dedication.

The 1970's was an era of liberal idealists in both American and Canadian capitals. John F. Kennedy, the first Catholic United States president, broke through a religious barrier. In Canada, the charismatic Prime Minister, Pierre Trudeau, sought national unity in the French and English speaking parts of Canada. English language lessons were required in schools in French-speaking Quebec, and English-speaking area schools taught French. Like many other countries, Canada has come to resemble a mosaic of many cultures living together.

Louise Fréchette

United Nations Deputy Secretary General
Canada

Louise Fréchette

[Address to the Third Annual UNA-USA Members Day,
United Nations, New York, 1 April 2000]

"RESPONDING TO GLOBALIZATION"

Ambassador William Luers, Ladies and Gentlemen, Friends,

It is a pleasure to join you today and to welcome such good friends and partners to the United Nations.

Much has changed since last year's UNA-USA Members Day, and much awaits us in the year ahead. Millennial fever continues with the Millennium Summit in September, the NGO Millennium Forum next month and the Secretary-General's Millennium Report. You have come together at a very opportune moment.

We have seen changes in the landscape of UN involvement around the world, especially in the area of international peace and security. One year ago, there was no United Nations peacekeeping operation in Kosovo, the people of East Timor had yet to be given a free say in their future, and the men, women and children of Sierra Leone were still being subjected to some of the most appalling human rights abuses the world has seen in recent years. Today, notwithstanding considerable obstacles, hope has returned to each place and United Nations peacekeeping operations are struggling to carry out a range of formidable responsibilities.

In Sierra Leone, a UN peacekeeping operation is working hard to secure a fragile peace, to ensure disarmament and demobilization, and to heal the deep psychological wounds of that brutal conflict. That operation may be the UN's largest in the world, and certainly faces an array of daunting challenges, but it is in Kosovo and East Timor that the tasks entrusted to the United Nations are truly all-encompassing. These two missions are qualitatively different from almost any other the Organization has ever undertaken.

In each place, the United Nations is the administration, responsible for fulfilling all the functions of a state – from fiscal management and judicial affairs to everyday municipal services such as cleaning the streets and conducting customs formalities at the borders. This is a new order of magnitude for an Organization that more customarily provides States with technical assistance in such areas rather than assuming complete responsibility for them. And it is a new order of magnitude for peacekeeping operations as well, making them extraordinarily complex and almost as dependent on civilian experts as on military personnel.

In Kosovo, the UN Mission is working in tandem with NATO and a range of European security and development partners, helping to rebuild Kosovo as a multiethnic society. This is a decidedly elusive goal given the well-publicized troubles the mission is encountering, but it is one to which we remain deeply committed. And in East Timor, the UN Transitional Administration is guiding the East Timorese towards their long-held goal of independence. This means re-building or building nearly everything – from infrastructure to institutions – virtually from scratch, since what little they had was mostly destroyed in the systematic violence of last September.

I should add that there was also, one year ago, no peace agreement for the Democratic Republic of the Congo. However, it remains unclear whether the parties involved are committed to transferring their differences from the battlefield to the negotiating table. Nonetheless, the Security Council has authorized the deployment of a United Nations peacekeeping operation if and when the right circumstances prevail. Should we reach that point, that operation, too, will be among the most complex and perilous we have ever undertaken.

Such operations have sparked a lively global debate about humanitarian intervention, about the moral responsibilities of the international community, and about the capacity of outsiders such as the United Nations to make a difference in internal armed conflicts and other humanitarian crises. The issues involved – human rights, democracy, solidarity with the less fortunate members of the global community – speak to American values and engage the American public. These are also operations in which Americans are involved – in some cases with troops, in others with material and logistical support, but in all cases through its assenting vote in the Security Council. None of these operations would have gone forward without the Council's approval, and none will achieve its aims without the resources and will of the Council and wider UN membership.

One should not take the approval of these missions as a sign that concerns about peacekeeping's effectiveness have disappeared. But their existence does signal support for the valuable role of peacekeeping as one of the diplomatic instruments the international community can deploy to help resolve conflicts. Given the failures and recriminations of the 1990s, that is no small thing.

Let me turn now from these highlights of the past year to the period ahead, and specifically the Secretary-General's Millennium Report. That report provides a comprehensive review of the challenges facing humanity at the dawn of the 21st century, and a range of recommendations for handling those challenges. You would not be mistaken in guessing that its starting point is globalization – the defining context of our times.

Globalization is not entirely new, of course; human beings have interacted across the planet for centuries. But today's globalization is different: in its extraordinary pace, its wide-ranging impact and especially in the technologies that propel it forward. As such it has major implications for both national and international governance. And while the hallmark of globalization – the integration of markets – may be leading to higher living standards on average, there are millions of people around the world who experience globalization not as an agent of progress but as a disruptive and even destructive force. Many more millions are completely excluded from its benefits.

Responding to globalization is the main challenge facing the international community – the leaders, states and civil society groups that must work together. If we are to realize the full potential of globalization, while minimizing the threat of backlash, we must learn to govern better, and how to govern better together. That is the broad nature of the challenge to which the Secretary-General addresses himself.

Since the founding of the United Nations, two inter-related goals have been paramount: helping the world's people achieve freedom from want and freedom from fear. I need not describe for you the terrible poverty in which over a billion of our fellow human beings exist, nor describe the damage inflicted on societies and individuals by armed conflict. In the past decade alone, five million people have died in wars, and many times more have been driven from their homes. Such numbers demand that we do better, and we can.

We must also acknowledge the urgency of attaining a third major freedom: the freedom of future generations to inherit an uncompromised natural environment with which they can meet their needs. Unfortunately, despite the Earth Summit, and despite important environmental agreements such as the Montreal Protocol on the Ozone Layer, we have continued to plunder the future. We are failing to protect resources and ecosystems, failing to invest enough in alternative technologies, especially for energy – and failing even to keep the debate alive. Peoples and Governments alike must commit themselves to a new ethic of conservation and stewardship.

The quest for these freedoms will take all our ingenuity, resources and will. Not least, the world's people will have to have in their hands a United Nations that works – a really useful instrument for tackling all these problems. That means a United Nations that knows how to take full advantage of new technology – especially information technology – and modern management techniques.

And it means a United Nations that interacts at every level with civil society – with NGOs, with academia, and the private sector – as well as its own Member Governments. Such partnerships are the new frontier of international action. They might take the form of NGOs working together through e-mail to advocate against landmines and for an international criminal court. You might see philanthropist entrepreneurs such as Ted Turner and Bill Gates donating truly remarkable amounts of money to UN agencies dedicated to fighting disease and protecting the environment. Or individual businesses might join the Secretary-General's "Global Compact" for greater corporate citizenship by doing what they can to end child labour and safeguard human rights. No matter what form these partnerships take, we are seeing what some have called an "associational revolution" that builds upon the state system, that increases our ability to get things done and from which there is no turning back.

The United Nations, for its part, has and will continue to have tiny resources by almost any standards of international organization. But its undeterred moral voice, allied with the new players on the international scene, creates enormous potential for the Organization to act as a catalyst and coordinator of efforts by others far richer, more powerful, more institutionally agile and less politically constrained than itself.

The United Nations has been grateful for your strong and consistent support over the years. We have an opportunity to steer the U.S.-UN relationship in a very constructive direction across the range of a broad agenda.

That agenda will be on display throughout the year – not only at the millennium events, but also later this month in New York at the review conference for the nuclear non-proliferation treaty; in April in Dakar at the world conference on education for all, which will focus on the education of girls, which many regard rightfully as the key to our hopes for the future and which is dealt with in some detail in the Secretary-General's report; in June at follow-up meetings for the Copenhagen summit on poverty, and at the Beijing Plus Five session on the advancement of women, which Angela King will tell you about shortly.

The time is right. The Millennium Report gives us a plan to rally around. All of us look forward to working with all of you. Thank you very much.

Angela King

$\mathscr{A}$ngela King has played a pivotal role in creating gender balance in the Secretariat of the United Nations; thus modeling gender balance for the world. She has an honors degree in History from the University College of the West Indies, and an MA in Educational Sociology and Administration from the University of London. She continued her education with further studies at New York University. In 1966 she joined the United Nations Secretariat from the Permanent Mission of Jamaica, one of the first two women foreign service officers posted after Jamaica joined the United Nations.

Early in her career, she worked in the Department of Economic and Social Affairs to prepare the Report of the World Social Situation. Later she served in the Branch for the Promotion of Equality Between Men and Women. She participated in the first United Nations Conference on Women, in Mexico City, 1975, and in the second United Nations Conference on Women, in Copenhagen, 1980. These conferences, the first of four, lay the groundwork in all areas of subsequent women's worldwide action.

A founding member of the ad hoc Group on Equal Rights for Women and a member of the Steering Committee on Improving the Status of Women in the Secretariat, King oversaw the appointments of the many outstanding women UN leaders, in areas of children, health, refugee care and human rights, among others.

From 1992-1994, King was on assignment as chief of mission of the United Nations Observer Mission in South Africa (UNOMSA), one of only two women who have headed a United Nations peace and security mission. In 1996-7, she directed the Division for the Advancement of Women, with responsibility for the follow-up to the Beijing Conference.

On March 1, 1997, Mr. Kofi Annan appointed Angela King to her present position as Special Advisor on Gender Issues and Advancement of Women with the rank of Assistant Secretary-General.

Editor's note: Clearly, the entry of women into decision-making positions in councils and legislatures does not happen automatically. The four United Nations Conferences on Women have been central to this change, but women have to "Take Beijing Home" to address problems at the local level. In June, 2000, the San Francisco Commission on the Status of Women hosted the 31st annual convention of NACW, the National Association of Commissions for Women. I was inspired to see how a vision for the future is translated into reality through workshops on such topics as 1) strategic planning and setting goals, 2) using new technology, 3) building coalitions, 4) using media and 5) fundraising. As in literacy campaigns, "each one teach one" works for leadership skills.

Angela King

United Nations Special Advisor on Gender Issues
and the Advancement of Women
Jamaica

Angela King

[Address to UN-USA member's annual meeting,
The United Nations, New York, June, 2000]

"GENDER BALANCE AT THE UNITED NATIONS"

I am truly delighted to be here today; to join distinguished colleagues in addressing a group which has been consistent in its efforts to understand and support the work of the United Nations. I would like to add my voice to those who have rightly saluted your decades-long association with the UN. And I also think it is right that I should bring you up-to-date on the forthcoming Special Session of the General Assembly which has as its theme "Women 2000: gender equality, development and peace for the twenty-first century."

As a result of the four major world conferences on women: Mexico City in 1975, Copenhagen 1980, Nairobi 1985, and the 1995 Beijing conference, the discourse on gender has taken hold among people from all points of the political spectrum, and in all groups; religious, secular and geographical.

This is because the UN's activities to promote the status of women have commanded the support of the most articulate and committed group in the world today. I refer to women, who constitute over half of the world's population, and who have become increasingly skilled in navigating the formidable obstacles they still encounter in international and national arenas. Women's groups are forthright in their determination to promote gender equality.

Through the joint efforts of the UN, its agencies, and Non-governmental Organizations (NGOs), gender equality has emerged as a major international priority. But concerted action is still required to ensure the advancement of women and to contribute to sustainable human development. The Session in June, 2000, will provide a blueprint for future action and contribute to deliberations at the Millennium Assembly in the fall.

Let us not forget that the UN's record on women has been among its most successful. One of the earliest bodies created by the fledgling United Nations was the Commission on the Status of Women which concentrated on the legal status of women in Member States and on preparing legislation and international conventions on the status of the women of the world.

The most important of these is the Convention on the Elimination of All Forms of Discrimination Against Women (CEDAW) which was adopted in 1979 and came into force two years later in 1981. Last October, the General Assembly adopted the Optional Protocol to the

Convention which has now been signed by 33 countries. It provides for two procedures: communications and inquiry which bring it into line with comparable existing procedures. Incidentally, thank you, UN-USA for the tremendous support in pushing the Senate to make the United States become the 166th State to ratify this very important Convention. Only 26 states in the world have not yet done so.

As for the UN itself, we have adopted a proactive policy to promote a gender perspective throughout the whole system by striving to meet the goal of 50:50 women and men in professional and higher level positions. We have achieved 38.6%. Despite the efforts of those who feel that women have achieved enough and perhaps have gone too far – much still remains to be done.

At the beginning of the twenty-first century, it is appropriate that we take stock of what has been done and what needs to be accomplished in the future. The last quarter of the past century has been marked by four world conferences on women, a cooperative effort by the United Nations, Governments, the international women's movement, non-governmental organizations and individual women and men towards the realization of gender equality and women's empowerment.

These conferences provided a forum for the development of new strategies to achieve equality, and to translate those ideas into government commitments and action. They have had a tremendous impact on the advancement and empowerment of women in all parts of the world. They have generated awareness, discussion and consensus on new goals and new methodologies in the achievement of gender equality and the elimination of discrimination against women.

They have also encouraged the development of a strong international women's movement, marked by the emergence of non-governmental organizations and advocacy groups particularly at the grassroots level. They have stimulated the development of international standards, and guidelines for putting national policies into place. They have also provided momentum for the creation of national machineries for the advancement of women.

Mr. Kofi Annan has said, "....from the birth of the United Nations, women have made skilful use of our organization as a platform to voice their demands for equality and non-discrimination. Women in government delegations and in non-governmental organizations recognize the power and the potential of this global forum."

Because the UN has provided such a forum, we can state the following:

- violence against women is now on every Government's agenda. It was the women of Latin America who first raised this issue resulting in the 1993 UN declaration against all forms of violence against women. Now almost all countries have enacted legislation on this issue, covering the home, workplace and society at large.
- harmful and traditional practices such as female genital mutilation, honour killings, and suttee, often used as an excuse for perpetuating the non-recognition of women's rights,

are now regularly discussed. Many countries now have legislation criminalising such practices.

- concern about the vulnerability of women in armed conflict has now been enshrined in the statute of the International Criminal Court. The ad-hoc Criminal Tribunals in Rwanda and the former Yugoslavia have brought indictments against those who used rape and forced marriages as weapons of war.

- women's tremendous role in conflict prevention, peacemaking and peace-building has been recognized by the Security Council in its momentous statement on International Women's Day, 8 March 2000, when it pledged to view women's role as integral to peace building.

Finally, in a departure from normal practice, in October 1996, the then Secretary General made a statement on the dire situation of women in a specific country, Afghanistan. Last month, on International Women's Day, for the first time in recent years, there was a celebration in Kabul of International Women's Day at which 700 Afghan women participated together with representatives of UN agencies.

At Beijing, 189 countries unanimously adopted the Declaration and Platform of Action. Designed as an agenda for women's empowerment, the Platform's emphasis was not only on achieving equality and eliminating discrimination but also on the integration of women as full and equal partners in all policy and decision-making processes.

Now we face the challenge of building on these achievements. As a means of achieving equality, the Platform advanced the concept of "gender mainstreaming" defined in 1997 as "the application of gender analysis to planning and policy making." Within the UN, this concept is a primary strategy in the design, implementation, monitoring and evaluation of policies and programmes in all spheres.

Governments have also committed themselves to this process and to consider all issues from both women's and men's perspectives. Many have reported success in including the gender perspective throughout all their budgets, policies, planning and decision-making.

The cycle of United Nations world conferences and summits has identified critical barriers to women's equal participation in decision-making and leadership. No doubt you are aware of these conferences, but it is right that I should remind you that at the Rio, Cairo, Vienna and Copenhagen conferences, on environment, population, human rights and development issues, all took account of women's perspectives.

The first critical barrier to women's progress is poverty. The majority of the world's poor are women. Yes, they are working in growing numbers, but in poorly paid and insecure jobs. Their capabilities continue to be undervalued; they increasingly work in the services sector, and they perform more part-time and unpaid work than men. They bear the brunt of the burden of poverty. Globalization is in some areas a further contributory factor.

When poor men and women are not so greatly burdened with the tasks of daily survival, they will become their own best advocates for social justice, political representation and peace and security in their societies.

Another critical issue for women is health care; the need for programmes to address maternal and infant mortality rates which remain unacceptably high.

This brings me to the question of education. Illiteracy continues to affect women disproportionately. Of the world's 130 million children who should be attending primary school, but do not do so, two-thirds are girls. We know that education has a critical role if not the most critical role in promoting women's participation in decision-making and leadership.

The 1995 Beijing Platform for Action has indeed begun a process which will lead to the achievement of equality for women sooner that many of us had hoped. Gender equality is achievable and it will happen well before the end of this century. We will know we have achieved it when, as Mary Robinson says, "women will be allowed to make mistakes and no one will blame it on their sex".

The practical implementation of UN decisions depends on the extent that citizens – men and women – are aware of the commitments made by their Governments on their behalf and of the extent to which Governments are accountable for the implementation of such commitments.

We want Governments to recommit themselves to the goals of the Platform for Action; we want them to state their national plans for the next five to ten years; and we need not only to meet the shortfalls in the 1995 Platform for Action, but also to address the new challenges that have emerged – globalization, the HIV-AIDS pandemic, and the question of water.

The United Nations is in a unique position to continue its tradition of success. We have no intention of failing the coming generations of girls and boys.

Her Excellency
Dr. Najma Heptulla

$\mathcal{M}$rs. Heptulla is an outstanding leader in her home country of India and on the world scene in the Geneva-based Inter-Parliamentary Union and in the United Nations. Born on April 13, 1940, she took a M. SC. University degree in Zoology in 1960, and at the age of 22, a doctoral degree in Cardiac Anatomy. She is married and has three daughters.

Her governmental posts include the office of Deputy Chairman of the Rajya Sabha (Upper House of the Parliament of India) from January 1985 to January 1986 and from 1988 to the present. As Special Envoy to the Prime Minister of India, she has traveled to Saudi Arabia, Iraq, Kuwait, Jordon, United Arab Emirates and Fiji. She is President of the Indo-Arab Society, and a member of the Board of Trustees of the India Islamic Cultural Centre, and a member of the Bombay City Social Education Committee.

Always interested in women's issues, she has been President since 1985 of the Indian Housewives Federation, and she has organized over a hundred seminars and several national level meetings for identifying and addressing women's problems. She is a member of the Maharashtra State Government Committee for the Status of Women, and was a special invitee of the World Women's Forum at Harvard University in 1997.

She participates actively in the work of the United Nations Development Programme (UNDP) as Founder President of the Parliamentarians' Forum for Human Development, and as a UNDP Distinguished Human Development Ambassador. She has been a member of the Indian delegation to the United Nations, participating in the Fourth World Conference on Women (Beijing, 1995).

In 1993, she chaired the Meeting of Women Parliamentarians, and was Vice President of the Specialized IPU Conference on "Towards Partnership between Men and Women in Politics", held in New Delhi in 1997. She has been a member of the Executive Committee of the Inter-Parliamentary Union since 1995 and Vice-President since 1997. In October 1999, she became President of the IPU Council.

Editor's note: Most people live under four levels of government: town, county, state (prefecture, province) and national. Each level exerts authority over legal documentation, taxes, freedom of movement and economic practices, among other activities. This mix of legal jurisdictions raises problems, and calls for tact and clarity. We now add the global level with regulations on environment, travel, mail, and increasingly, human rights. Mme. Heptulla gives an example of effective work on many levels from local to international, with special attention to the needs of women. In this millennium year, the IPU published a fascinating survey of the world's women parliamentarians, and a map/poster showing the percentages of women in parliaments.

Her Excellency Dr. Najma Heptulla

President, Governing Council of the Inter-Parliamentary Union
President, Conference of Presiding Officers of National Parliaments
India

Her Excellency
Dr. Najma Heptulla

[United Nations Millennium Summit, 6-8 September 2000 United Nations, New York]

"THE INTER-PARLIAMENTARY UNION
AND THE UNITED NATIONS"

Distinguished co-Presidents of the Millennium Summit, Mr. Secretary-General, Excellencies, Ladies and Gentlemen,

I am honoured to take the floor as the President of the Conference of Presiding Officers of National Parliaments and on behalf of the oldest international organization, the Inter-Parliamentary Union, to present to you the outcome of a unique and historically compelling event held in this hall from 30 August to 1 September in cooperation with the United Nations, with the participation of some 150 Presidents of Chambers from 140 countries.

This first ever Conference of Presiding Officers of National Parliaments truly represents the commitment of representatives of the peoples, the Parliaments, to work ever more closely with the United Nations to ensure that the twenty first century is a century without fear, without deprivation and want, a century that allows for the fullest development of the inherent potential of each and every human being. That will be real globalisation.

Mr. Secretary-General, we thank you for your very inspiring address on that occasion. Your messages will be reciprocated through our actions. After intense debate, we unanimously adopted a Declaration encapsulating our parliamentary vision for international cooperation at the dawn of the third millennium. It sets out the main challenges facing our societies and expresses our political resolve to successfully overcome them, through international cooperation. It also contains recommendations on the role of parliaments in a reformed multilateral cooperation system.

Mr. President, Parliaments stand firmly behind the United Nations and this support is both political and practical. Whether we belong to the majority or the opposition in our parliaments, we are committed to offering the necessary political backing to the UN as the cornerstone of the international cooperation system. We are also committed to allocating the resources which the United Nations and the other intergovernmental institutions need to accomplish their noble mission.

We are unanimous in identifying a democratic deficit in the United Nations and the intergovernmental regime at large. If UN decisions are to interpret the concerns and aspirations of the peoples and if international agreements are to effectively find their way to our national realities, parliament, as the institution which legitimately represents society in its diversity and is accountable to it, should have a greater say in the international cooperation process.

No doubt it is for you, governments, to negotiate at the UN. Surely, our main role as legislators is to translate into legislative and budgetary provisions the agreements reached internationally by you. Yet it is in the wider interests of all, and certainly in the interests of democracy, that we be involved in the process in its early stages and not exclusively in the implementation phase. Intergovernmental organisations would also become more accountable and would be perceived as more transparent by the people if we were better informed about and associated with their action as the people's representatives.

We are happy to note that the Millennium Declaration that this August gathering will adopt calls for a strengthening of cooperation between the United Nations and the national parliaments, through their world organization, the Inter-Parliamentary Union, that I have the honour to represent. I and my colleagues will do all that is in our power, and attempt much that is beyond, to give concrete shape to your call.

We are determined to see to it that the necessary work is done at the national level and especially within our national parliaments so that action can be taken to develop the parliamentary dimension of the international cooperation for which we are calling. To create this new partnership, parliaments intend to act in close consultation with you, governments and with the intergovernmental organisations.

Internationally, the Inter-Parliamentary Union is a unique instrument to relay the views of our parliaments to the intergovernmental system. This is why we can no longer accept its current status at the United Nations and we look forward to identifying with you a status for the IPU which is commensurate with the constitutional status of parliaments and with IPU's mission as our world organisation.

Mr. President, We were concerned that two of our fellow Presiding Officers were prevented from participating in our Parliamentary Summit. The denial of visas to them runs counter to the spirit on which the IPU and the UN are founded and is contrary to the principles of democracy underlying the functioning of parliaments. Furthermore, it calls into question our ability to meet at the United Nations in New York to express the support we intend to offer it. I therefore call on you all and the host country urgently to help us find a solution to such problems.
Thank you.

Gro Harlem Brundtland

A practicing medical doctor who became, at 41, the first woman and the youngest Prime Minister of Norway, Gro Harlem Brundtland has worked in medicine, the environment and politics at the highest levels of national and international life. Born in Oslo, Norway, on April 20, 1939, she followed in the footsteps of her father, Dr. Gudmund Harlem, a specialist in medical rehabilitation much in demand after the second World War. When she was ten, the family moved to the United States when he received a Rockefeller Fellowship. He later worked in Egypt for the United Nations.

By 1963, Dr. Brundtland had a medical degree from the University of Oslo, and in 1965, an MA degree in public health from Harvard University. For the next nine years, she had responsibilities for children's health in the Ministry of Health and as Director of Health Services for the schoolchildren of Oslo. Her dedication and enthusiasm resulted in an invitation to become the government's Minister of the Environment. Understanding the close connection of human health and the environment, she undertook the career change.

Her introduction to political life had also started early. At the age of seven, she was enrolled as a member of the Norwegian Labour Movement in its children's section, and has been a member ever since. During the 1970's, she gained a reputation as a skilled politician and was internationally recognized as an expert in environmental issues. She was appointed Prime Minister of Norway in 1981 and she won re-election in 1986 and 1990. She served as head of the Norwegian government for ten years.

In 1983, the United Nations Secretary General invited her to chair the World Commission on Environment and Development. In April, 1987, the Commission published its groundbreaking report, "Our Common Future," which brought in the concept of "sustainable development." Its recommendation for a world summit meeting resulted in the United Nations Conference on Environment and Development (UNCED) in Rio de Janeiro in 1992.

Dr. Brundtland was elected to her present position as Director-General of the World Health Organization of the United Nations and took office on July 21, 1998.

Editor's note: Dr. Brundtland's energy and "no-nonsense" tone is striking in her keynote address at the Cairo Conference on Population and Development in September, 1994. The world listened to her call for reproductive health care for women to be seen as a human right. The next year, at the Beijing Conference, I listened to a panel of Palestinian women doctors talking enthusiastically about the maternity clinics they were setting up. Six years later, Dr. Sadik, in her talk that follows, is able to show how much the discourse about women has changed in regard to population and development. The change is due in part, I believe, to Dr. Brundtland's fearless and challenging 1994 speech.

Gro Harlem Brundtland

Director, World Health Organization
Norway

Gro Harlem Brundtland

[Keynote Address to the International Conference on Population and Development, Cairo, Egypt, 5 September 1994.]

"SEXUAL AND REPRODUCTIVE HEALTH CARE"

*L*et us turn from the dramatizing of this Conference which has been going on in the media, and focus on the main issues. We are gathered here to answer a moral call to action. Solidarity with present and future generations has its price. But if we do not pay it in full, we will be faced with global bankruptcy.

This conference is really about the future of democracy, how we widen and deepen its forces and scope. Unless we empower our people, educate them, care for their health, allow them to enter economic life on an equal basis and rich in opportunity, poverty will persist, ignorance will be pandemic and people's needs will suffocate under their numbers. The items and issues of this conference are therefore not merely items and issues, but building blocks in our global democracy.

It is entirely proper to address the future of civilization here in a cradle of civilization. We owe a great debt to President Mubarak and the people of Egypt for inviting us to the banks of the Nile, where the relationship between people and resources is so visible and where the contrast between permanence and change is so evident.

We are also indebted to Mrs. Nafis Sadik and her devoted staff, who have provided the conference preparations with intensive care and inspiration.

Ten years of experience as a physician and 20 as a politician have convinced me that improved life conditions, a greater range of choice, access to unbiased information and true international solidarity are the sources of human progress.

We now possess a rich library of analysis of the relationship between population growth, poverty, the status of women, wasteful lifestyles, consumption patterns, – of policies that work and policies that don't and of the environmental degradation that is accelerating at this very moment.

We are not here to repeat it all, but to make a pledge. We make a pledge to change policies. When we adopt the Plan of Action, we sign a promise – a promise to allocate more resources next year than we did this year to health care systems, to education, family planning, and the struggle against AIDS. We promise to make men and women equal before the law, but also to rectify disparities, and to promote women's needs more actively than men's until we can safely say that equality is reached.

We need to use our combined resources more efficiently through a reformed and better coordinated United Nations system. This is essential to counteract the crisis threatening international cooperation today.

In many countries where population growth is higher than economic growth, the problems are exacerbated each year. The costs of future social needs will be soaring. The penalty for inaction will be severe, a nightmare for ministers of finance and a legacy which future generations do not deserve.

But the benefits of policy change are so great that we can not afford not to make them. We must measure the benefits of successful population policies in savings – on public expenditure on infrastructure, social services, housing, sewage treatment, health services and education.

Egyptian calculations show that every pound invested in family planing saves 30 pounds in future expenditures on food subsidies, education, water, sewage, housing and health.

Experience has taught us what works and what does not.

With 95 per cent of population increase taking place in developing countries, the communities that bear the burden of rising numbers are those least equipped to do so. They are the ecologically fragile areas where current numbers already reflect an appalling disequilibrium between people and earth.

The preponderance of young people in many of our societies means that there will be an absolute increase in the population figures for many years ahead, whatever strategy we adopt here in Cairo. But the Cairo Conference may significantly determine, by its outcome, whether global population can be stabilized early enough and at a level that humankind and the global environment can survive.

It is encouraging that there is already so much common ground between us. The final programme of action must embody irreversible commitments towards strengthening the role and status of women. We must all be prepared to be held accountable. That is how democracy works.

It must promise access to education and basic reproductive health services, including family planning as a universal human right for all.

Women will not become more empowered merely because we want them to be, but thorough change of legislation, increased information and by redirecting resources. It would be fatal to overlook the urgency of this issue.

For too long women have had difficult access to democracy. It cannot be repeated often enough that there are few investments that bring greater rewards than investment in women. But still they are being patronized and discriminated against in terms of access to education, productive assets, credit, income and services, decision-making, working conditions and pay. For too many women in too many countries, real development has only been an illusion.

Women's education is the single most important path to high productivity, lower infant mortality and lower fertility. The economic returns on investment in women's education are generally comparable to those for men, but the social returns in terms of health and fertility by far exceed what we gain from men's education. So let us pledge to watch over the numbers of school-enrollment for girls. Let us watch also the numbers of girls that complete their education and ask why if the numbers differ, also because the girl who receives her diploma will have fewer babies that her sister who does not.

I am pleased by the emerging consensus that everyone should have access to the whole range of family planning services at an affordable price. Sometimes religion is a major obstacle. This happens when family planning is made the moral issue. But morality cannot only be a question of controlling sexuality and protecting unborn life. Morality is also a question of giving individuals the opportunity of choice, of suppressing coercion of all kinds and abolishing incrimination of individual tragedy. Morality becomes hypocrisy if it means accepting mothers suffering or dying in connection with unwanted pregnancies and illegal abortions, – and unwanted children living in misery.

None of us can disregard that abortions occur, and that where they are illegal, or heavily restricted, the life and health of the women is often at risk. Decriminalizing abortions should therefore be a minimal response to this reality, and a necessary means of protecting the life and health of women.

Traditional religious and cultural obstacles can be overcome by economic and social development, with the focus on enhancement of human resources. For example Buddhist Thailand, Moslem Indonesia and Catholic Italy demonstrate that relatively sharp reductions in fertility can be achieved in an amazingly short time.

It is encouraging that the International Conference on Population and Development will contribute to expanding the focus of family planing programmes to include concern for sexually transmitted diseases, and caring for pregnant, delivering and aborting women. But it is tragic that it had to take a disaster like the HIV/AIDS pandemic to open our eyes to the importance of combating sexually transmitted diseases. It is also tragic that so many women have had to die from pregnancies before we have realized that the traditional Mother-and-Child health programmes, effective in saving the life of so many children, have done too little to save lives of women.

In a forward looking plan of action, it therefore seems sensible to combine health concerns that deal with human sexuality under the heading "sexual and reproductive health care". I have tried, in vain, to understand how that term can possibly be read as promoting abortions or qualifying abortion as a means of family planning. Rarely, – if ever, – have so many misrepresentations been used to imply a meaning that was never there in the first place.

I am pleased to say that the total number of abortions in Norway stayed the same after abortion was legalized, while illegal abortions sank to zero. Our experience is similar to that of other countries, namely that the law has an impact on the decision making process and with the safety of abortion – but not on the numbers. Our abortion rate is one of the lowest in the world.

Unsafe abortion is a major public health problem, in most corners of the globe. We know full well, all of us, that wealthy people often manage to pay their way to safe abortion regardless of the law.

A conference of this status and importance should not accept attempts to distort facts or neglect the agony of millions of women who are risking their lives and health. I simply refuse to believe that the stalemate reached over this crucial question will be allowed to block a serious and forward-looking outcome of the Cairo conference – <u>hopefully</u> based on full consensus and adopted in good faith.

Reproductive health services not only deal with problems that have been neglected, they also cater to clients who have previously been overlooked. Young people and single persons have received too little help, and continue to do so, as family planning clinics seldom meet their needs. Fear of promoting promiscuity is often said to be the reason for restricting family planning services to married couples. But we know that lack of education and services does not deter adolescents and unmarried persons from sexual activity. On the contrary, there is increasing evidence from many countries, including my own, that sex education promotes responsible sexual behaviour, and even abstinence. Lack of reproductive health services makes sexual activity more risky for both sexes, but particularly for women.

As young people stand at the threshold of adulthood, their emerging sexuality is too often met with suspicion or plainly ignored. At this vulnerable time in life, adolescents need both guidance and independence; they need education as well as opportunity to explore life for themselves. This requires tact and a delicately balanced approach from the parents and from society. It is my sincere hope that ICPD will contribute to increased understanding and greater commitment to the reproductive health needs of young people, including the provision of confidential health services for them.

Visions are needed to bring about change. But we must also let our vision and commitment materialize through allocation of resources. The price tag for the program that we are here to adopt has been estimated at somewhere between 17 and 20 billion dollars per year.

The really hard work begins when ICPD is over. It is a major challenge to translate the new approach and objectives into implementable programmes. Norway will continue to participate in a dialogue with our bilateral and multilateral partners. We are pleased to see that important donors such as the United States and Japan are now increasing their support to population issues. Other countries should follow suit. Hopefully, Norway will soon be joined by other donor countries fulfilling the target of allocating at least 4% of ODA* to population programs.

It is also important that governments devote 20 per cent of their expenditures to the social sector and that 20 per cent of ODA is allocated towards eradication of poverty.

In order to meet the cost requirements of this programme of action, however, another long-standing target needs to be fulfilled, the 0.7 per cent of GDP* for ODA. The so-called "donor fatigue", again attributed to the general budgetary problems of the industrialized world, will certainly not facilitate this challenge. Budgetary priorities and allocations are being fought for by national Governments every year. And the 1 per cent-and-above allocation to ODA which Norway has been able to defend over the last 15 years or so, does not materialize without serious political work. Our work would be greatly facilitated by two factors: 1) that other donor countries begin approaching the target of 0.7 per cent, and 2) important both in Norway and, maybe to the whole donor community, that this conference like other world conferences proves by its outcome that we are truly committed to a new and more real solidarity with the world's poor and underprivileged – they who are without a voice, and without a choice.

Population growth is one of the most serious obstacles to world prosperity and sustainable development. We may soon be facing new famine, mass migration, destabilization and even armed struggle as peoples compete for ever more scarce land and water resources.

In the more developed countries the fortunate children of new generations may delay their confrontation with the imminent environmental crisis, but today's new-borns will be facing the ultimate collapse of vital resource bases.

In order to achieve a sustainable balance between the number of people and the amount of natural resources that can be consumed, both the peoples of the industrialized countries and the rich in the South have a special obligation to reduce their ecological impact.

Changes are needed, both in the North and the South, but these changes will not happen unless they stand the test of democracy. Only when people have the right to take part in the shaping of society by participating in democratic political processes will changes be politically sustainable. Only then can we fulfill the hopes and aspirations of generations yet unborn.

I take this privileged opportunity to summon and challenge this Conference to answer its responsibility towards coming generations. We did not succeed in Rio with regard to population. Cairo must be successful – for earth's sake and humanity's sake.

ICPD means International Conference on Population and Development

*ODA means Official Development Assistance, a tax on countries able to contribute to the United Nations Assistance programs to needy countries.

*GDP means Gross Domestic Production, the statistical base for ODA rates.

NOTES

Dr. Nafis Sadik

$\mathcal{D}$r. Sadik,* educated in medicine and public health in Calcutta, Karachi and at the Baltimore City Hospital and Johns Hopkins, was born in 1929 in the Indian state of Uttar Pradesh, before the partition of British India in 1947 into Muslim and Hindu-majority nations. As a girl in a Muslim home, she was lucky, she said, because she was prodded into being assertive and choosing her own career. When her future husband, Azhar Sadik, went to ask for her father's permission to marry her, her father told him that she would want to work. Mr. Sadik, who later gave up his job to follow her to the United Nations, replied, "Don't I know it; she's told me a hundred times."

The year 2000 will mark the end of her 14 years as executive director of the United Nations Population Fund. She has concerns about its financial future, largely because of significant reductions in American contributions, only partly restored by the Clinton administration. Japan, the Nordic countries and the Netherlands are now the fund's leading contributors.

Dr. Sadik said that her Muslim upbringing and background in the developing world has enhanced her credibility in dealing with reluctant or suspicious governments. "We decided that we must promote the idea of population as a development issue." Dr. Sadik also tried to avoid emotional debates over cultural values by casting practices like female genital mutilation as a public health issue for women.

Dr. Sadik said that while there is much work to be done, it can now be done in a new atmosphere of frankness. The fact that concepts such as female reproductive rights, rape, and the sex trade can be discussed openly "is an indication of massive, massive change in thinking." Many women health experts say that the most significant shift of gears in dealing with issues of population came at the 1994 International Conference on Population and Development in Cairo, which Dr. Sadik directed.

Editor's note: The critical relationship between population and development impressed me deeply when I met a woman from the San Blas Islands in Central America whose fingers were worn down to the first joint. She had picked beans in the field from the age of 8, "often with tears running down my face." Her mother died at age 30 with 15 children.

*Adapted from Barbara Crossette's article "Working for Women's Sexual Rights" in the New York Times, October 2, 2000 page A8, and unpublished material sent by Ms. Crossette.

Dr. Nafis Sadik

Executive Director, United Nations Population Fund
Pakistan

Dr. Nafis Sadik

[Speech given to the Commission of Population and Development, United Nations, New York, 27 March 2000.]

"A Comprehensive Approach to Population and Development"

Mr. Chairman, Ladies and Gentlemen,

*I*t is a pleasure for me to address the thirty-third session of the Commission on Population and Development. Since we met last year, two important events closely followed by demographers everywhere took place: the observance on 12 October, 1999 of the birth of the six billionth person on this planet and the convening on 30 June-2 July 1999 of a Special Session of the General Assembly on the review and appraisal of the implementation of the Programme of Action of the International Conference on Population and Development. Both events are significant in their own right.

The arrival of the six billionth baby was heralded as a day of celebration and a time for reflection. It was a time to look back at our accomplishments – more people are living longer and healthier lives than at any time in history – and to reflect on how we should proceed to ensure that we can adequately provide for at least the basic human needs of all the earth's inhabitants.

The successful conclusion of the Special Session marked the end of the ICPD+5 review process that began in 1998. The process focused primarily on policy changes and operational experiences at the country level in order to draw out lessons learnt, identify constraints encountered and recommend key actions to overcome them. It was characterized by broad United Nations system-wide participation and the involvement of a wide range of civil society organizations. United Nations Population Fund's *Report of the Secretary-General on the Special Session of the General Assembly for the Review and Appraisal of the Implementation of the Programme of Action of the International Conference on Population and Development* examines the review process and discusses the outcome of the Special Session.

The thirty-second session of the Commission on Population and Development, which acted as the Preparatory Committee for the Special Session on ICPD+5, is to be commended for its tireless efforts – through two formal sessions and one informal session, some of them lasting long into the night – to negotiate the document that was presented to the General Assembly for adoption at the Special Session.

The review demonstrated that the ICPD goals are still valid and that much progress has been made in advancing these goals. Many countries have embraced and strengthened the recognition of reproductive and sexual rights through policy changes. Many have taken steps to integrate population concerns into their development strategies. And many have added new components to reproductive health services while also improving access to them.

At the same time, the review revealed that much greater and urgent action is needed in such areas as reduction of maternal morbidity and mortality; addressing the sexual and reproductive health needs of adolescents; the prevention of HIV/AIDS; and the provision of reproductive health care to women and adolescents in emergency situations. It also noted the need for a pragmatic approach when dealing with adolescents.

The adoption by consensus of the document, *Key Future Actions for Further Implementation of the ICPD Programme of Action*, by the General Assembly Special Session, is testimony to the seriousness and importance placed on these issues by all countries. It validates the comprehensive approach to population and development articulated in the Programme of Action, affirms the ICPD goals and provides a set of interim benchmarks for achieving the ICPD goals. Among the benchmarks are:

- By 2005, the 1990 illiteracy rate for women and girls should be halved, and by 2010, the net primary school enrolment ratio for children of both sexes should be at least 90 per cent;

- By 2005, 60 per cent of primary health care and family planning facilities should offer the widest achievable range of safe and effective family planning methods, essential obstetric care, prevention and management of reproductive tract infections including STDs, and barrier methods to prevent infection; 80 per cent of facilities should offer such services by 2010, and all should do so by 2015;

- At least 40 per cent of all births should be assisted by skilled attendants where the maternal mortality rate is very high, and 80 per cent globally, by 2005; these figures should be 50 and 85 per cent, respectively, by 2010; and 60 and 90 per cent by 2015;

- Any gap between the proportion of individuals using contraceptives and the proportion expressing a desire to space or limit their families should be reduced by half by 2005, 75 per cent by 2010, and 100 per cent by 2015. Recruitment targets or quotas should not be used in attempting to reach this goal;

- To reduce vulnerability to HIV/AIDS infection, at least 90 per cent of young men and women, aged 15 to 24, should have access by 2005 to preventive methods – such as female and male condoms, voluntary testing, counseling, and follow up, and at least 95 per cent by 2010. HIV infection rates in persons 15 to 24 years of age should be reduced by 25 per cent in the most-affected countries by 2005 and by 25 per cent globally by 2010.

A serious lack of financial resources remains one of the chief obstacles to full implementation of the ICPD Programme of Action. This fact is described in more detail in UNFPA's *Report of the Secretary-General on the Flow of Financial Resources for Assisting in the Implementation of the Programme of Action of the International Conference on Population and Development*. Most developing countries are not in a position to generate the required resources to implement the ICPD goals. Donor funding, which hovers at the $2 billion mark, is far below the target of $5.7 billion agreed to at Cairo. Both increased political will and a renewed commitment to mobilize the necessary resources are essential to the further implementation of the Programme of Action which, in turn, will contribute to the advancement of the broad population and development agenda.

The Special Session urged Governments and the international community to promote additional mechanisms to increase funding for population and development programmes in order to ensure their sustainability. Donors were encouraged to significantly increase official development assistance (ODA) for other elements of the Programme of Action, including the improvement in the status and empowerment of women.

With the Beijing+5 Special Session only a few months away, it is fitting that the theme of the thirty-third session of the Commission is "population, gender and development", a theme which picks up on one of the main topics of the Cairo document: gender equality and equity and the empowerment of women. The ICPD recognized that the empowerment of women is a highly important end in itself and a key to improving the quality of life for everyone. This was further articulated in the ICPD+5 review.

Many issues on which agreement was reached during ICPD+5 will come up during the Beijing Special Session. It is up to all of us to ensure that, during this Session, the agreements on these issues remain intact, as they are crucial for the health and well-being of humanity.

As you begin your deliberations on the topic of gender, population and development, you can, with considerable satisfaction, take note of the progress achieved thus far and urge the international community to redouble its efforts to build a society in which all individuals – men and women, girls and boys – can enjoy the peace, human security and dignity that they truly deserve.

Thank you.

NOTES

Sadako Ogata

$\mathcal{M}$rs. Ogata assumed office as the United Nations High Commissioner for Refugees on 18 February 1991. She was elected to this post by the United Nations General Assembly and re-elected since then. She will retire at the end of 2000.

Sadako Ogata was born on 16 September 1927 in Tokyo. She graduated from the University of the Sacred Heart in Tokyo in 1951. In 1953, she received an MA in international relations from Georgetown University, Washington, DC and in 1963, a Ph.D. in political science from the University of California, Berkeley. From 1965 to 1974, she lectured in international relations at the International Christian University and at the University of the Sacred Heart, also in Tokyo. From 1974 to 1976, she served as Associate Professor, Diplomatic History and International Relations, at the International Christian University in Tokyo.

From 1978 to 1979, she began her association with the United Nations as Chairman of the Executive Board of UNICEF. Also during 1978 and 1979, Mrs. Ogata was Envoy Extraordinary and Minister Plenipotentiary at the Permanent Mission of Japan to the United Nations, having served as Minister there from 1976 to 1978. From 1982 to 1985, she was Representative of Japan on the United Nations Commission on Human Rights. In 1990, she was the Independent Expert of the United Nations Commission on Human Rights on the Human Rights Situation in Myanmar in 1990.

Her distinguished academic career through the 1980's includes service as a professor and Director at the Institute of International Relations, and as Dean of the Faculty of Foreign Studies at Sophia University in Tokyo.

Professor Ogata has published a number of books on diplomatic history and international relations as well as numerous articles. A national of Japan, she is married and has a son and a daughter.

Editor's note: In her teen years, Sadako Ogata witnessed the bombing of Tokyo in World War II. The plight of war refugees left an indelible impression and a determination to be of service. As the efficient and respected United Nations High Commissioner for Refugees, she has filled one of the most difficult jobs in the world, managing, with an inadequate budget, to care for some fifty million people dispossessed because of war. In the 1950's, after the second World War, it was thought the refugee problem would end, but it is much larger now.

Sadako Ogata

United Nations High Commissioner for Refugees
Japan

Sadako Ogata

[Address given in New York City, USA , July 18, 2000]

"PROTECTING PEOPLE ON THE MOVE"

Ladies and Gentlemen,

*I*t is a pleasure to be with you this afternoon. I would first of all like to thank the Center for the Study of International Organization and especially its Executive Director, Ed Luck, for organizing this event.

My talk today concerns the challenges of protecting people on the move, and I wish to focus in particular upon the plight of internally displaced people. I believe this is an area where the United Nations and all other concerned actors must join forces more effectively for people who are in need and at risk.

The Increasing Complexity of Forced Displacement

The United Nations High Commission for Refugees' (UNHCR) work protecting refugees began fifty years ago. The nature of refugee movements – their causes, composition and consequences – has changed radically since then, as has the international humanitarian response. Keeping the asylum door open has never been easy, even during the bipolar Cold War period. But we are now seeing new and more complex models of displacement.

Asylum-seekers fleeing persecution, human rights violations and violence tend to travel alongside people seeking better economic opportunities, those uprooted by natural disasters and others. They often come from the same countries, travel the same routes, hold the same false documents and use the services of the same criminal trafficking and smuggling networks.

As a result, asylum and irregular migration have become seriously confused in the public mind, and refugees have become stigmatized as people trying to circumvent the law. Disturbingly, some governments have even questioned the continuing relevance of the 1951 Convention relating to the Status of Refugees, the universal foundation of refugee protection.

But traditional refugee movements across international borders have always been only one aspect of forced displacement. While global refugee numbers have remained more or less stable recently, the number of people displaced within borders has risen dramatically. **The available data are fragmentary, but the most reliable estimates indicate that some 20 to 25 million people may be displaced internally around the world, roughly twice the number of refugees.**

The phenomenon of mass internal displacement has presented a different sort of challenge to the notion that "refugees" are a distinct group of international concern. Ambassador

Holbrooke returned from a tour of Africa late last year outraged by the absurdity of either aiding or abandoning people depending upon whether they fall on one side or the other of an unmarked border. He called for much greater attention and support for internally displaced people, whom he termed "internal refugees."

Refugees Remain Distinct

At the risk of sounding pedantic, I must take issue with this term "internal refugees." Blurring the distinction between refugees and internally displaced people may suggest to some that protection provided within borders is equivalent to the international protection afforded to refugees. Refugees benefit from an international legal regime for non-nationals on the soil of another state. That regime is supervised by a responsible and accountable international organization, UNHCR. We must take care not to undermine the unique legal status of refugees or to lend encouragement to strategies aimed at containing displacement. The asylum door has to remain open for people who genuinely need protection.

The Human Cost

Having made this qualification, I want to echo strongly Ambassador Holbrooke's basic message: **we are failing internally displaced people**. By "we" I mean to include governments, the United Nations system and the broader humanitarian community. The scale of suffering and the human cost are staggering.

I have just undertaken my 31st mission to Africa since becoming High Commissioner in 1991. My visits have spanned a very difficult decade for tens of millions of people caught up in the continent's many conflicts. The number of people helped by UNHCR in Africa has risen from 950,000 in the early 1960s to 3.7 million in 1980 to nearly 6.3 million today. Yet this massive figure reflects only a fraction of the total number of people in need of protection and assistance in Africa. In the Democratic Republic of the Congo alone, for example, an estimated 1.8 million people are displaced internally. Tens of thousands of them lead a nightmarish existence, roaming the bush in search of food, safety and temporary shelter. **Caught between multiple warring parties and constantly shifting frontlines, many of these "forced nomads" do not even know who is fighting, let alone why.** Thousands have been trapped, wounded or killed in the crossfire.

Beyond this horrific toll are the millions of unseen casualties – people who continue to suffer and die in darkness and silence. A recent study by the International Rescue Committee estimates that 1.7 million people have died in the eastern Democratic Republic of the Congo from war and violence, as well as from infectious disease, malnutrition and other indirect consequences of the conflict. Children less than two years of age account for a third of the excess deaths. People rendered more vulnerable by displacement undoubtedly have suffered disproportionately.

I have focused upon the Congo, where the situation is most acute and least attended. But I could have drawn equally appalling examples of forced displacement and misery from other parts of Africa, Asia, Europe and the Americas. In too many of these situations, displacement is not merely a consequence of conflict, but its very objective. **The governments responsible for protecting the rights and well being of internally displaced people are often the cause of their predicament, as they pursue calculated strategies aimed at changing the ethnic map of the country or gaining control over economic resources.**

The bottom line is that millions of people uprooted by conflict are exposed to extreme hardship, violence and death. What help they do receive is selective, uneven and, in many cases, inadequate.

UNHCR's Role

UNHCR's role in situations of internal displacement is not new. Our operational involvement with internally displaced people spans some thirty years. My Office currently provides protection and assistance to some five million people displaced within borders in a range of operations from Colombia to Kosovo and the Caucasus.

The General Assembly has acknowledged UNHCR's particular expertise and has encouraged our efforts in situations of internal displacement, most notably in General Assembly resolution 48/116 of 1993. The General Assembly's recognition of UNHCR's work with internally displaced people has been reinforced by a series of Conclusions issued by our Executive Committee, as well as by specific requests for our involvement from the Secretary-General.

It is important to note that UNHCR's involvement with internally displaced people usually begins with a request for assistance from the concerned government. Our work in the Balkans, for example, began with a 1991 request from the Government of the Federal Republic of Yugoslavia. UNHCR's programmes for internally displaced people in Colombia, the Russian Federation and Sri Lanka followed similar government requests, as have our recently initiated activities in Angola and Eritrea. Each of these governments recognized the constructive support UNHCR can offer in meeting the protection and assistance needs of citizens caught up in a displacement crisis. I would like to emphasize that State consent is, and will remain, essential for UNHCR's entry into a situation of internal displacement.

Refugees and the Internally Displaced

With the proliferation of civil conflicts, UNHCR increasingly finds that refugees and internally displaced populations are mixed together. In Liberia, for example, UNHCR faces a situation where Sierra Leonean refugees are living alongside internally displaced Liberians, returning Liberian refugees and other war-affected people who have managed to remain in their homes. In such circumstances, targetting refugees alone presents both moral and practical dilemmas. The humanitarian needs of the refugees and other vulnerable groups may be indistinguishable and impossible to address in isolation.

Refugees and internally displaced people are often the same people seeking to go home to the same places. Where new states are born from conflict – as in the former Yugoslavia and East Timor – the distinction between refugees and the internally displaced may be unclear. Their solutions also are usually linked. Creating conditions for displaced people to return home in Bosnia and Croatia, for example, frees up the housing they occupy and enables refugees to repatriate.

I believe that these examples show the importance of dealing with refugee flows and internal displacement in a comprehensive way. Refugees and internally displaced people are legally distinct, but UNHCR's operational strategies and solutions must be coherent and inter-linked. Comprehensive approaches to displacement can even have a positive preventive impact on refugee flows – not by preventing people from seeking asylum, but by making asylum an option rather than a necessity.

What Can UNHCR Offer?

Ladies and Gentlemen,

We all recognize that the problem of internal displacement is complex and the needs are huge. You may legitimately ask, what does UNHCR have to offer in dealing with situations of internal displacement? At UNHCR, we pride ourselves on being an operational agency – one that is able to translate humanitarian concerns and principles into concrete action in the field. I believe that our main strengths lie in three areas:

First, UNHCR understands how decisions on humanitarian assistance activities – from camp design to the distribution of relief – can undermine, or promote, protection objectives. Care and skill are needed to avoid creating dependency and unequal gender relationships, and empowering the wrong people. Equally, properly designed assistance programmes can be an important tool of protection. For example, UNHCR enhances the protection of refugee women by systematically encouraging their participation in the design, implementation and monitoring of projects intended for their benefit.

UNHCR's second key strength is that we know how to make the connection between legal principles and practical protection in the field. Refugees and internally displaced people are not protected by the same legal framework. The most important rights of internally displaced people are those they ought to enjoy as citizens. They are also protected by the relevant principles of international humanitarian law and human rights law, as reflected in the Guiding Principles on Internal Displacement.

But UNHCR's practical approaches to protection in the field are relevant to both groups. We protect people by maintaining an active presence, developing a detailed knowledge of local conditions, identifying communities and individuals at risk and bringing attention to their needs. We rely upon the competence and courage of our field staff, particularly their ability to build and manage relationships with hostile authorities and local communities under difficult circumstances. A well-timed intervention made by a UNHCR field officer may be the last line of defense against forced relocation, arbitrary detention, the military recruitment of children and other human rights violations.

As a third point, I would emphasize UNHCR's special expertise in achieving solutions for forced displacement. This is perhaps our greatest comparative advantage. UNHCR is presently coordinating repatriation and reintegration operations in countries as diverse as Afghanistan, Bosnia, East Timor, Liberia, Myanmar and Somalia. We understand how to analyze and address barriers to return – from strengthening arrangements for physical security and meeting basic humanitarian needs to legal issues such as registration, documentation, amnesties and the recovery of property rights.

We also have experience devising low-key, community-level approaches to building confidence, promoting dialogue and strengthening local mechanisms for conflict mediation and resolution. The Bosnian and Rwandan Women's Initiatives, for example, have played a pioneering role in breaking down barriers by bringing women from different ethnic backgrounds together in project teams.

The Challenges Ahead

Ladies and Gentlemen,

I welcome the current debate over internally displaced people, but I think the focus has been too narrowly concentrated upon the quality of the international response and the allocation of responsibilities among the key agencies. All the talk of mandates and comparative advantages obscures certain hard realities. I want to close my remarks by bringing these broader challenges back into view.

First, as I have said many times, forced displacement is a humanitarian consequence of underlying political, social and economic problems. Humanitarian action undertaken without regard for these root causes or a determination to achieve real solutions is doomed to fail. The efforts of UNHCR and other humanitarian actors can only buy time for peace initiatives to bear fruit. They can only help to bridge the gap until longer-term reconstruction and development efforts get underway.

Sustained international political engagement is necessary. Otherwise, humanitarian intervention offers no solution. It can even be counterproductive, because humanitarian efforts create an illusion that someone is dealing with the problem. And lives of humanitarian workers are placed in unnecessary peril to no lasting effect.

The international community has usually been much too slow in seizing the openings presented by peace settlements and much too timid in their support, particularly in Africa. The same governments that insist humanitarian workers put their lives on the line to relieve suffering in the Congo and Sierra Leone do not seem prepared to ensure that well-armed, well-trained peacekeepers are alongside them on the frontlines. We must be aware that protecting and assisting people in the midst of an internal conflict situation is complicated and dangerous. We cannot operate without agreed ground rules and guarantees regarding humanitarian access and security for our personnel and logistics operations.

Finally, I will be blunt. Making a real difference for internally displaced people will require a very substantial and sustained commitment of resources. We will need people, equipment, relief goods and logistical support; and we will need money. The cost will be especially high in Africa.

Having said this, I must say that UNHCR presently exists in a "zero sum" budgetary environment. Any expansion of our activities requires equivalent reductions somewhere else in the world. Donor governments encourage us to budget for actual needs, rather than on a realistic assessment of our funding prospects. Few donors, however, are willing to back that up with the resources required. UNHCR faces increasing difficulties meeting the basic needs of refugees, who are our primary and mandatory responsibility.

Any greater involvement with internally displaced people will be contingent upon reliable assurances of adequate additional funding. A test case has already been thrust upon us. Last week, UNHCR launched an appeal seeking $23 million to provide food and shelter for Eritreans displaced by the recent war with Ethiopia, including $13.2 million for people displaced within Eritrea. What tangible support can we expect?

UNHCR has also initiated a new programme to protect and assist internally displaced people in three provinces of Angola. The United States Government has stepped forward and indicated its willingness to contribute $2 million. Will others follow its example?

...Other humanitarian crises are on the horizon around the world, and massive internal displacement is a factor in most. Will the political will and funding be there?

The renewed interest in internal displacement within the political organs of the United Nations and in many capitals gives us a window of opportunity to strengthen our common response to this growing problem.

But without more serious attention to the broader context of forced displacement and a stronger, more determined political and financial commitment, the spotlight currently focused on the plight of internally displaced people will soon dissipate into darkness once again.

Thank you.

Rosario Robles

$\mathscr{I}$n her trademark black Jeep, Rosario Robles Berlanga, Mexico City's first woman Mayor, presents an image of no-nonsense cheerfulness as she whizzes between official functions. She became Mayor on September 29, 1999 when the mayor Cuauhtémoc Cárdenas resigned to run for President. She had previously, in December, 1997, been elected to the position of General Secretary, the second in charge of that huge city and federal district.

Within five months of taking office, Mayor Robles had faced down a wildcat protest of two thousand people blocking traffic and threatening to paralyze the city's downtown area. With her blend of efficiency and approachability, she managed to reduce by seventy per cent the number of protests that had occurred in the same period of the previous administration.

She has bridged the gap between the remote power structure and the electorate by encouraging initiatives like the Citizen Participation Law. The city's recently reformed Electoral Code requires political parties to put forward women candidates in a proportion of at least 30%. She published her own personal financial record to dispel the traditional assumption that politicians are not accountable to the public.

From 1988-1993 she was Director of the Women's Section in the Executive Committee of the Workers Union of the National University of Mexico. In 1989, she participated in founding the Democratic Revolution party. By 1997, as an official of the party, she coordinated the "Sun Brigades" which were fundamental to electoral success in the same year.

An economist by profession with a teaching credential in rural development from the National University of Mexico, she has been a columnist, a researcher on issues of poverty and gender, and the author of books on the Mexican rural economy. In the legislature, she presided over the Commission on Social Development at the time when basic agreements were established for electoral reform within the constitutional context.

Born 44 years ago in the Federal District to parents Marla del Rosario Berlanga and Francisco Robles, she is married to Julio Moguel, an economist. They have a 16 year old daughter, Mariana.

Editor's note: How appropriate it is to have a big city mayor who is a specialist in rural poverty and development! The influx of rural people to the major cities of the world brings special problems in housing, mental and physical health and community life. We have seen examples from Bombay to Manila of the plight of people trying to create communities in the worst areas, even on the garbage heaps. Mayor Robles' success in handling problems such as street peddling and family violence comes in part from her expert understanding of the newly displaced poor trying to survive in the city.

Rosario Robles

Mayor of Mexico City; Federal District
Mexico

Rosario Robles

[Address to the forum "Parliament of Mexican Women" given in the House of Representatives, International Women's Day, March 7, 2000]

"GOVERNING MEXICO CITY"

Good afternoon.

I would like to thank the Commissions on Equity and Gender of the House of Representatives and the Senate for their invitation to me to reflect on the experience of governing Mexico City, one of the biggest cities in the world, with problems that are very complex, very diverse, with years of deterioration, which began to turn around as of December, 1997.

It's very important, this process of reflection being carried out this week by the country's parliament itself, concerning women's participation. March 8th, International Women's Day, is very relevant because we still participate in a legislature from the past; we still need a Commission on Equity and Gender. We need to reflect on the problematic situation of women, on the insertion of women into public life, into political life. I congratulate you for this action because it speaks to the process of cultural transformation now happening in our society.

We are talking about promoting a new relationship between the sexes. We are talking not only about women occupying more spaces, more presence in the places where decisions are made, in legislative spaces, in executive bodies, but also how this greater presence might translate into a cultural change, a new relationship to the inner core of society, in which men and women can fully guide the destinies of our homeland.

I believe the fact that women are confronting the tasks of legislating and governing speaks to this great advance, but also to the enormous responsibility of demonstrating that we are capable of doing it and that our decisions are beneficial to the majority.

I support specific policies which must be put into action by governments, so that the inequality we have lived with for years can start being compensated for and balanced out little by little. That is what affirmative action is for; it can provide measures to compensate for that imbalance and begin to reach that equality.

Having a woman at the head of Mexico City's government is an affirmative action. I believe it is truly significant; first, many women feel like participants in this process. They feel this as a triumph, but not a personal one. Likewise, I don't see it as a personal triumph, but as a triumph for women, for the enormous struggle that we have all engaged in to secure these positions, through our different political parties.

I believe that women see it that way, and feel it that way, as a triumph for us all and as a kind of mirror in which they see themselves reflected, and as a hope opening up that we women can gain access; that it's not impossible for us to be governing cities like Mexico City. Neither is it impossible that, at some point, we'll be governing a country like our own.

A second effect is that it challenges not only those of us women who assume these responsibilities. It's a double challenge to govern this city and, at the same time, to govern it <u>as a woman</u>. The public official is always on trial, but it's also a challenge for the public to assume that women govern. I am speaking not only about the groups of working people; but also about social, political and economic managers, whom one has to relate to. Perhaps a true story will give you a clear picture.

When I held the second most important position in the city government, as deputy mayor, Sr. Cárdenas, the mayor, once asked me to do him the favor of communicating with the manager of the Metro union, to sort out some issue. I called his office, but he [the union manager] didn't want to speak to me. He said he didn't speak with women, and, furthermore, why should he speak to a woman about labor questions, since what would I know about labor questions. This says a lot, also, about how we have to start building this equity; not just from one side, but from both sides.

I wasn't intimidated; I called him again. I spoke to him, and insisted that he respond. I said to him: "I come from a union. For six years I was the manager of a union like the one at the National Autonomous University of Mexico. I have fought all my life for the labor rights of workers. And so, of course we have a lot to speak about, you and I."

Obviously, it is not a problem of any one person in particular. It's a cultural problem, I repeat, in which all of us have to transform ourselves. Not only women, but also our companions, men, in this new vision of a pluralistic society.

Here is another anecdote: This morning I was reading an article by a columnist, where suddenly he says: "...and Chayo something..." [referring to Rosario Robles by a nickname], and I wondered: would he write 'Ernesto,' or would he say 'Neto,' or would he say 'Vicente,' or would he say 'he.' No, I don't think so, I think it has to do with the fact that I'm a woman that he dares to say 'Chayo' and not 'Rosario,' because I don't think that in relation to the President of the Republic or any other governor, he would address them in this manner.

So, this is what we live with, and this is why we must not only rise up to fill these positions, but also to contribute, from these positions, to bringing about changes in social relations between men and women, changes which stem from a fundamental recognition that society is diverse. It is pluralistic, not only politically, but in its social composition: ... because we are women ... because there are men ... because there are young people ... because there are indigenous people ... because there are handicapped people...

Thus, our obligation as women when we govern is precisely to contribute to the recognition of these differences by creating policies that generate this vision of equality. At the same time, we must create ways of conducting ourselves in the government and ways of doing politics which also contribute to these cultural changes.

For example, women are associated with certain stereotypes. When we are decision-makers in the government, we are Margaret Thatcher. Why? Why is it that a man making a decision is totally normal; they don't say that he's hard, that he's inflexible because he makes a decision. As women in professions, we participate in the making of decisions, and if we make them energetically, firmly, then it means we're "hard, inflexible." Why? Because we are associated with other values; they associate us always with other kinds of attitudes, and not with decision-making.

Therefore, I believe it is essential to change these stereotypes, through the presence of women in politics, so that the images of women given to our children and young people of the new generations will be totally different. Formerly, when we looked at political coverage, on television or in a newspaper, we used to see only images of men. Today, our sons and daughters see images in which there are women and men. This also begins to transform the vision of women in politics.

I also believe – and it's very important to point this out – in a city like ours, as enormous and problem-burdened as it is, that the decisions that are made carry with them a gendered vision, a gendered perspective.

How should women govern? It's not that we're different; we must also destroy those myths. "Women are more honorable, women are more responsible, women are more dedicated." No. I believe this depends on the individual. It also has to do with the particular task and many other things.

But what is certain is that when women govern, when we make policy, we indeed can run the government in a different way. We can act with a firm hand, but in a gentle manner. We can, above all, apply a maxim which for us is very important: <u>tolerance</u>, because we have always struggled from this perspective, of opening up spaces, of being perceived as different. So, when we have responsibility in the government, we are obligated to promote the participation of women.

And I would like to say, with much pride, that in the Electoral Code of the Federal District, as a result of the all the discussions we had in the work groups for political reform, it became mandatory for political parties to place women on their electoral lists in a proportion of at least thirty percent. This is not a recommendation: it is an obligation established by the Electoral Code itself.

The Citizen Participation Law, which created neighborhood committees, established that women and men must participate equitably. And in many of the neighborhood committees, elected by a universal, secret vote last year, the coordinating positions are held by women. Why?

Because the neighborhood committee is directly linked to citizen demand, to the daily life of the citizens, to their problems with garbage, safety, services, land use, etc.

In this city, the women are the ones who participate most in these types of problem areas. It is the women who always fight for the services, who lead the demand for safety because these issues have to do with their own families and their own children. Women are the ones who fight so that bigger buildings are not constructed, or so that the use of the land is respected, etc.; they are always concerned with this daily dynamic and this citizen struggle.

Women participate actively in the neighborhood committees in Mexico City. This participation, I believe, is beginning to change the face of the city.

We are also targeting equality in the workplace. In Mexico City, there are still companies that require a woman to prove she is not pregnant when she takes the job. There are companies that still fire women for being pregnant. Some companies even advertise as a requirement that you be a male. This is unconstitutional. It goes against the constitutional principle of the right to work, an egalitarian principle for men and for women, who should not be subject to obstacles of this nature. But there are no mechanisms as yet that impose sanctions on these discriminatory practices.

In the recently reformed Penal Code of the Federal District, discrimination was included as a practice which must be punished. We also implemented an area specifically giving attention to women workers. Cases are received on a daily basis of women who are victims of discriminatory practices in their work. The two most frequent complaints concerning the working woman are, first, discriminatory practices and, second, sexual harassment in the workplace. But the instruments for dealing with these problems are still very inefficient because there are no legal processes for sanctioning conduct in the workplace.

It is through the Penal Code and the penal procedure that as individuals we can take action. And I hope we will soon be able to file lawsuits against a company for discriminatory practices in our country, to prosecute them and receive compensation for damages. This responsibility falls upon you, the legislators, because this is very important and governments are endowed with stronger instruments for defending women in the workplace.

Likewise, regarding violence, we have carried out very important reforms, and you have participated in the latest reform in this matter. In the Federal District's Penal Code and the Penal Procedure, we managed to establish a very important policy for protecting the victim: beginning to change the vision in many penal codes of protecting the victimizer, and moving it toward protecting the victim, above all in the case of sexual crimes.

We not only established more severe sanctions for sexual crimes, but we eliminated the face-to-face confrontation between the victim and the victimizer. That reform that has been carried out recently, last year in the Legislative Assembly of the Federal District.

Face-to-face confrontation was a major problem, when boys or girls were victims of sexual harassment or aggression or rape; especially as we know, much of this takes place within the home. A significant portion of this violence comes not from strangers, but from somebody who is known. Therefore, reporting this to the police becomes much more difficult when they are boys or girls being abused by the head of the family or the cousin, or the uncle of somebody in the family. In these cases, face-to-face confrontation was particularly complicated. It has now been established that the victim can have access to other types of mechanisms, through cameras, etc. to identify the victimizer without direct confrontation.

The need for such measures was evident in the case of the young girls raped in Tláhuac. Since the law allowed a face to face confrontation of 7, 8 or 9 hours, despite the presence and support of women's organizations, even as co-adjudicators so the girls could fully exercise their rights, it made an extraordinarily difficult situation.

This law is one of the most important recent reforms in Mexico City, as well as the Women's Support Centers, and ten new Domestic Violence Shelters. The shelters have hardly got their working papers in order, and yet they are constantly receiving women, above all victims of these violent practices within the home.

At present, we are debating a proposed reform in the Federal District's Civil Code which would establish the full exercise of human rights within the family. This would be legislated for the protection of the family, in order to rule, from the civil angle, against these violent practices which are so common.

I would also like to point out that we put in motion a program with 3,000 health educators, who visited 7,000 homes, house by house, in Mexico City's poorest neighborhoods. Our focus was on health and the detection of certain illnesses, and on the families' living conditions. As expected, we found inadequate housing, unemployment, poverty. But for us, it was truly an extraordinary experience, when in the groups that we formed with these health educators, the number one problem that they reported was <u>violence</u>. In other words, they didn't bring us surprising news about poverty, about houses with tin roofs that were falling in; these are things we already know. Instead, they told us violence was the biggest problem.

The second biggest problem was addiction, which is also a product of family disintegration, poverty, the lack of horizons, of opportunities, which unfortunately is very present among young people, and now also among young boys and girls. I was very struck by the impotence of these young people in dealing with these problems because their training and abilities are fundamentally in other directions.

Quickly we had to orchestrate different sorts of programs for the care of community mental health, in order to approach these particular problems.

This difference of views speaks to us about the complexity of society and about this great fracture in the social fabric, and about fragmentation at the bottom of society, and which we cannot attack with traditional public policies. Instead, we have to begin to arm ourselves with policies which are more complex, which attend to the range of problem areas we are facing.

Clearly, these 3,000 educators, all women, all health educators, showed us something about this "women's vision" – this perspective we often have, the fact that necessarily or consciously we do have a gendered vision, and that particular vision allowed them to perceive the community situation in a much more complex way.

In the area of health care, we have been fully engaged. The best health services are concentrated in Mexico City. However, it ranks second-highest in female mortality for cervical-uterine cancer. In other words, the city that has more health services than any other region continues to have the highest mortality rates for cervical-uterine and breast cancer. And in this city, women continue to die in childbirth due to hemorrhaging or a toxemia not treated in time. These are things we cannot permit.

As a consequence, first, we need a the total reorientation of health services, above all reproductive health, with quality services; second, health resources, especially resources that have to do with the early detection of cancer. Important efforts have been made, but we should double the efforts in this area because there is a problem we must confront and solutions we must find.

We have our Health Centers, which care for women in a formal manner, so to speak. Many women in Mexico City have access to Social Security [the national health service], because they work in companies that have Social Security, or work in the public sector or in decentralized organizations. They have the right to ISSSTE [national health services]. But many others do not have any type of services. And so, through the Health Centers, we are trying to provide this service.

We also put in motion a system, which in my opinion is quite a new thing and has very positive results because it reaches to where the women actually are, and that is the Mobile Medical Units for the detection of cancer. These Units are fully equipped for the detection of cervical-uterine cancer, for taking pap smears, with specialized doctors, trained nurses. They go to the places where the women are, entrances to schools, public markets, places where there is a concentration of females, that is where the medical unit goes.

There they create public awareness so that women can have a pap smear done or she can have a breast examination, with the objective of checking for cancer. Many women who have used these services have later been rerouted through the official health services, precisely as a result of the diagnostic tests that we have done there. We have also created nine Dysplasia Clinics, not only for detecting but also for treating women with cervical-uterine cancer. These are some of our priorities which reflect our commitment toward women who are at the forefront of the City.

When women have this enormous opportunity to govern, we have the great opportunity to take in hand those things we have fought for: the equity which we have always talked about, the possibility to put our dreams into reality, and with what we may legislate, into practice, even with all the budgetary and social limitations. But one cannot govern if one does not at least start putting into motion these kinds of programs which we have always struggled for.

I know, having myself been a legislator, and now being in the government, that an alliance has always existed among the women of all political parties; and women from the civil society have always fought for better policies.

I know that having more women in the government, in a greater proportion both in cabinets and as governors, will be beneficial so that women-oriented public policies – our gender vision – will begin to be a reality in our country.

Thank you very much.

(Translation from Spanish by Linda Ribera)

NOTES

Benedita da Silva

*E*verything could have gone wrong. Who would have bet on the success of that black girl born March 11, 1942 in the *Favela* (Brazilian word for shanty-town or slum) Praia do Pinto? Who would guess that, 57 years later, the ex-*favelada* would become the vice-governor of the State of Rio de Janeiro, after being elected councilor, twice federal Deputy and then Senator, with an expressive voice that made her one of the most outstanding leaders in her national party?

Her family came to Rio de Janeiro from the northern mining center Minas Gerais. They settled in Praia do Pinto, but moved away soon to Morro do Chapeu Mangueira, in Leme, where she still lives. This is the place where Benedita developed her extraordinary capacity of persuasion. And she did it in social work, starting as a community school teacher, where she used the Paolo Freire method to teach children and adults to read and write.

Her next step was to found and lead the *Associacao das Mulheres do Chapeu Mangueira* (Chapeu Mangueira Women's Association) where she acquired experience later put to use in the Women's Department of FAFER (*Favela* Associations' Federation of the State of Rio de Janeiro) and at the *Centro de Mulheres de Favela e Periferia* (Favela and Outskirts Women's Center), organizations that she helped to set up and to run. With all that, she still had time and energy to study, and graduated in Social Sciences and Social Assistance.

Benedita's political life symbolizes the new moment of Afro-Brazilians' ascension which began in the 1970's. During her career, she has insisted on affirming her identity, based on the triad that is a synthesis of exclusion in Brazil – black, woman, *favelada* – understood everywhere as <u>race, gender and class</u>, which she changed into a positive element. Her successful parliamentary initiatives reflect the claims of the social movements which support her: elimination of discrimination against women, blacks and native indians; defense of the environment; protection of children and the fight against South African *apartheid*.

Her tireless struggle could have made of Benedita a bitter and dogmatic militant if it weren't for her being heiress of the best African traditions. That tradition made it possible for a long-suffering and humiliated people to create the rhythms and dances that cheer the planet and, in the political world, to assert themselves and make themselves be heard. That's the way she faces the challenges while now in charge of social action in the administration of Governor Anthony Garotinho. Benedita da Silva is sure this is only the beginning of her walk with the people toward future victories.

Benedita da Silva

Vice-Governor, State of Rio de Janeiro
Brazil

Benedita da Silva

[Speech given, October 3, 1996, in Rio de Janeiro]

"A NEW POLITICAL ROLE FOR WOMEN"

*I*n the recent elections, women achieved a new and important political position which will contribute to the process of equal rights in our society.

We understand that this is a decisive action in the fight of Brazilian women for a stronger political role, a demonstration of our maturity on questions of equal rights between men and women. As a consequence, our increasing representation in Congress and in municipal executive power will help the growth of social justice and democracy.

Before the Second World War, women held one per cent of positions in the Parliament even though they were more than fifty per cent of the voters. Progress was very slow. Currently, the Senate has 6 women out of 81 senators; 34 women out of 513 deputies to the lower house and something like 3 per cent of all the town councils in the whole country.

Politics has always been a masculine space, built historically by men and for men. We are now living in a time of change, and we seek political representation appropriate to our importance in the social fabric. We want a greater participation of women not only in the National Congress, but in municipal bodies, in the executive positions of unions, renters organizations, forums of city dwellers; finally, to have a voice in society for the practical realization of a better life for the people.

We want to take up community issues, with participation of our daughters and sons, in the context of the familiar and domestic problems of life. The daily life of women has been transformed as much by the access to education, by work outside the home as by reproductive choice and control. It is a struggle for a public role that has been denied us long enough.

The full exercise of citizenship entails the right of representation to a voice and a turn for women in public life, but also to dignity in daily life, the right to an education, to health, to security, and a family existence free from trauma.

We understand that the women's vote brings with it this double necessity: equality in the political system and in civil life. Democracy will only exist when equal rights without prejudice of sex, race, color, class, political and religious belief, physical condition or age will be guaranteed by equal access in streets, platforms, assemblies and palaces.

Inequality between men and women did not arise in the present. It goes back to pre-historic time. In Brazil, statistics reveal that women have access to only 25% of all the wealth produced in the nation; even less in rural areas. Of every ten families, three have women heads of households; women who live alone with their children. The salary difference between men and women varies a lot according to the occupation. We must find a way to change this percentage. It is so unfair to women!

The number of women in management is small. Although out of 100 workers, 40 are women, they are rarely able to climb the work place hierarchy. Hardly 10 per cent of director or top manager positions are filled by women, a percentage that falls to 4 per cent in the larger companies.

Life expectancy for women is greater than for men. In Brazil, women live on average 69 years, and men 63 years. This distinction gives women some advantage. As we see in the primary school grades, we women take to school better. But white women can hope for a better life than black women, who have less assistance.

Maternal mortality in Brazil is one of the highest in Latin America. We have two hundred deaths for each hundred thousand live births. We estimate that in Brazil, 5,000 women will die each year from compilations of childbirth; during labor or post-partum. There are more childbirth deaths in Brazil than abortions although it is estimated that each year 1.5 to 2 million clandestine abortions happen in conditions of risk.

The greatest cause of death for women comes from circulatory problems and uterine cancer, illnesses for which diagnosis is easy and a cure is certain if treated in time. But poor quality health service and lack of specialized care has turned women's reproductive health care to death.

The largest increase in AIDS cases is now among women. In 1983, for 31 male AIDS cases, there was one female case. Surprise of surprises! In 1995, we had one female infected for every three males. In Sao Paulo in 1993, AIDS was the principal cause of death for women between the ages of 20 to 34.

A gain in legislative and executive positions for women will contribute much toward social justice in Brazil. A woman in a high government position will have an awareness of social problems and of what happens in the family day to day.

The upsurge of women has reached as well to international organizations like the United Nations, which instituted in 1975 The International Year of the Woman. In Brazil, that date was very important, for it brought a rebirth of our fighting spirit.

We propose a great effort to increase women's influence, in particular, our presence in politics and institutions, which for us is a great challenge. We are engaged! Ready to fight! We have faith that in this way we will make possible a better future when the rights of women will not be insulted; a world where we will value each human being; each one having as the highest priority life, that divine gift, the cause and reason of our existence.

Fusae Saito Ohta

Fusae Saito Ohta was born in the Hiroshima Prefecture on January 26, 1951. She took a degree in economics from the University of Tokyo. Immediately after her graduation in 1975, she began her career in the Ministry of International Trade and Industry [MITI] in the Industrial Policy Division. A few years later, employed in the Personnel Division of the Minister's Secretariat, she traveled to California and was a Research Fellow at Stanford Research Institute in Palo Alto, California, United States. On her return, she rejoined the Industrial Policy Bureau of MITI.

Throughout the decade of the 1980's, she built her career gaining experience in various divisions of MITI. She became Deputy Director of a number of government agencies with responsibility for an impressive range of issues: Industrial Policy, Urban Areas Development, Energy Policy Planning, Land Planning and Regional Development, among others.

By 1988, she had become the Director for Industrial Relations in the Corporate Affairs Division of MITI's Industrial Policy Bureau. Until 1997, she held several Director positions in Housing and Consumer Goods Research for MITI, and was Director-General in the Policy Planning Department of the Kansai Bureau of International Trade and Industry.

She entered elective office in July, 1997, as vice-governor of Okayama Prefecture.

After another year at MITI as Deputy Director-General for Commerce and Distribution Policy, she ran for the office of Governor of Osaka Prefecture, an election she won in February, 2000.

Fusae Ohta

Governor, Osaka Prefecture
Japan

Fusae Ohta

Address to the Osaka Prefectural Assembly
Osaka, Japan, September 28, 2000 (Abridged)

At the opening of this September plenary session of the Assembly, I would like to talk about the problems we are facing and how we can cope with them. I would like to have your understanding and cooperation.

We are approaching the closing of the 20th century. We built our prosperity, but in the meantime, all sorts of structures and systems with which we have tried to catch up and overtake other countries into this century are suffering something like "metal fatigue." Although we do see a dim light at the end of the tunnel, it is very difficult to break through the shell of a sluggish economy, complex urban problems and the crisis of local finance, by using the conventional formulas.

And these problems have appeared with utmost intensity in Osaka. For example, when we look at economic activity after the bubble collapsed, Japanese recovery continues to move slowly. In Osaka, the indexes of individual consumption and productivity are lower than the national average. Unemployment levels are serious compared to other prefectures. The use of information technology "IT" in Japan is one step behind the other industrial countries, and Osaka is even more behind than the average of Japanese regions.

So when we look at the Osaka Prefectural Government's financial condition, comparing with 1989 when the revenue from corporate taxes peaked, corporate taxes are now less than half of what they were then, at 400 billion yen. The ordinary balance ratio has been over 100% for six consecutive years. The fiscal stasis is extremely rigid. In the fiscal year 2000, we fell short of 530 billion yen in financial resources, and we used to have 430 billion as the basic fund. Now that is exhausted. We are really in a financial crisis.

Turning to social issues, we find that the population is concentrated in age because of the past high growth period, and we evolved rapidly towards an aging society with very few children. As a result, we must move quickly to deal with this problem. This was another problem, clearly related to urban life, that appeared in Osaka before other prefectures. We need to create a flowing current that will take us to a reborn Japan. All the modern problems we face in Osaka appear as the epitome of Japan today.

We must not only clear away the after-effects of the economic bubble, but also reform the social and economic system which lasted for fifty years after the Second World War. In other words, from Osaka, we must create the source of our vitality for the 21st century. This is the task for Osaka to perform. The Osaka Prefectural Government administration itself must change. For the coming century, we will continue our ceaseless efforts to change the foundations and structures, and I want you to understand that in that process, we might have to ask the citizens to endure hardships to arrive at a new era – sometimes that is unavoidable.

Next, I would like to talk about my basic views on how we can deal with major issues, focusing on the themes I want the Assembly to deliberate on.

FIRST: INDUSTRY REBUILDING

We live in a very competitive world. In order to regain the vitality of our local economy and connect to the rest of the world and to live well, the community itself has to be engaged with the industrial policies to support new enterprises. In this, Osaka should be a leader. To re-establish a vibrant Osaka, I would like to devote all my strength to working on our new program, "Osaka Industry Rebuilding Program."

The effectiveness of the program will happen by the private sector doing its part. The government will work hard to create the foundation for achieving the goals of the program by involving individual citizens and small enterprises and all others in the private sector as the main players. First, I will promote the start of new enterprises as well as promote new business for small, already existing businesses to work for the basic goal of Osaka's rebirth. In the spirit of "If we create a new business, it should be in Osaka," we will reduce taxes for new industries. We will build the TLO [Technology Licensing Organization] and include an "Angel's Fund" and other diverse financing measures in our project menu. We will encourage the information and communication, biotechnical, environmental, health and welfare service sectors and the new industrial sectors that will become the driving force of industrial rebuilding. I want to create promising initial markets for industries, especially IT, [information technology], which is a "key to prosperity" in the 21st century. I have just made "The Osaka IT Declaration" for progress in IT.

We would like to carefully monitor IT development and lead its further development in all of Osaka. Moreover, to move this program forward, I will be in close contact with the City of Osaka, and start a committee of people from industry, universities and governments, "The Osaka Industrial Rebuilding Evaluation Committee," which will set numerical targets and evaluate our progress appropriately. For this program, we estimate a cost of more than 100 billion yen including both from the government and the private sector. In September, I appropriated a supplementary budget for immediate use. Next year, we will go to a larger scale.

SECOND: NEW REVENUE RESOURCES AND TAXATION AUTHORITY REVISION

The government needs to establish flexible but stable financial structures to cope with different kinds of administrative problems in our maturing society under the present tax system.

Even prefectures in metropolitan areas such as Osaka are being forced to depend on the local allocation tax. I think that the distribution of tax revenue between the national and the local governments must change.

To achieve a radical reform of our local administrative and financial systems, first, I would like to provide for stable financial resources by transferring the tax revenue from the national to the local level for income and sales taxes.

To make various independent and comprehensive programs in the metropolitan area possible, I have asked the national government to establish a "Subsidy for Urban Renewal." I have presented this proposal to the national government because the transfer of financial resources from the national level has not yet happened. It is a realistic financial measure for a transition period, and we are making this proposal in focused areas to bring a breakthrough. Given this opportunity, I will work harder to appeal to the national government for the reform of our administrative fiscal system to create a secure financial base of support, possibly in cooperation with other prefectures located in metropolitan areas.

We also have to think about how to exercise our right to impose taxes autonomously, the freedom for local taxation. I think it is very important to do this "Osaka style," which means that everyone pays an equal share on the basis of a "wide but thin" local tax to complete our administration reform. We will ask all people in community to pay according to how much they will benefit.

The "Osaka Tax System Reform Plan," is a result of the examination of our tax system. And, as I have said before, I propose reforms such as tax revenue sources transfer, increased local control of taxation, raising of the per capita rate of corporate inhabitant tax, conversion of automobile tax into "green" tax, a tax system to enable us to promote and invite new enterprises.

Among these taxes, the per capita rate system of corporate inhabitant tax is for the community social cost to be burdened widely and thinly. With corporate inhabitant tax on an income base, corporate inhabitant tax payment per company has been decreasing, and is now at 40% of its peak level. This tax is supposed to be used for the costs of the community. Because of the decreased corporate tax, the Osaka Prefectural Government's financial base is in crisis. In the meantime, we have to deal with urgent issues adequately, such as reviving Osaka industries.

After deliberation, I submitted a proposal to double the standard tax rate of the per capita rate portion of corporate inhabitant tax, which I believe to be acceptable. [Corporate inhabitant tax: a tax on corporations setting up business within the prefecture.] Small corporations will be exempt. From now on, we will argue for these taxes more often in the Assembly and with Osaka residents. At the next February Osaka Prefectural Assembly plenary session, I will announce the new tax schedules.

THIRD: ADMINISTRATIVE FINANCIAL REFORM

To become financially healthy, the key thing is administrative and fiscal reform. I will work diligently to achieve this reform. We will deal with administrative problems with the help of "outsourcing." We can't avoid arguing about the so-called "3rd sector" development project.

Now, in many self-governing local communities, people cannot find solutions to their problems. The problems are very difficult, and whichever road we choose, there will be a lot of unavoidable pain. However, it is my mission to lighten the burden for the next generation. I will tackle these problems and not put them off for the future.

To achieve administrative and financial reform, we should not forget to make use of IT; we must not ignore the wave of the information technology revolution now moving rapidly on a global scale. I will make the necessary improvements according to the "Osaka IT Declaration." We will be "an electronic government" which offers convenient service to Osaka residents, a service that is appropriate and up to date.

The realization of electronic government will make a major change in the relationship between the people of Osaka and the administration. Using the personal computer, we can communicate wherever and whenever.

We will make use of IT in the areas most closely connected to people's lives, such as health and welfare. We will work hard to provide high quality service to correspond to people's needs. I will also make the "paperless" administrative office revolution applying electronic application networks procurement and more efficient office systems.

To do this, I will soon provide one personal computer to every government employee. We will swiftly promote the "Comprehensive ITization" of the entire Osaka Prefectural Government with the leadership of an "IT Promotion Task Force."

IT can be just a tool, that may be true in one aspect, but there is no doubt that the introduction of IT will show us the inefficiency of old customs, administrative waste, and IT will lead to a drastic change of government employees' awareness.

FOURTH: HUMAN DEVELOPMENT

It is through people that the "Osaka Industry Rebuilding" program and the reconsolidation of the prefectural government will be accomplished. In any period of time, fostering human resources that can sustain and advance Osaka is always a key issue.

My goal in particular is to foster leaders who can be a strong influence in the future of Osaka so we can open up our present closed condition.

By leaders, I do not mean dominating, authoritarian figures, but people who have good personalities and creativity, who earn the trust and respect of the public, and who can overcome problems and be firm leaders. For this purpose, I think it is important to bring such leaders into various fields. I would like to say, "Let's raise the children who are our wealth – together let's raise them well." I would like the cooperation of people not only in the field of education, but also in business and community groups. I would like to be engaged in "putting each person in the center" in all fields.

However, the recent series of occurrences of violent cases by 17 year olds should be a warning for us. When we look at the condition of our youth now, we cannot help feeling a sense of crisis about our future. I will take urgent measures such as to give attention to their parental and psychological care, with the help of appropriate prefectural institutions. We must carry out effective preventive measures against youth delinquency.

Next, we have to address actions that threaten individual life and dignity; child abuse, domestic violence, sexual harassment, stalking. Any kind of violence should not be tolerated, and these acts in particular are painful to contemplate. Each one violates human rights; we cannot live with this. To remedy the problem, we will create new, effective programs and also work diligently with those now in place.

In the 21st century, our traditional views and social systems will undergo major changes. Among them will be the relationship among villages, towns and cities, as I have already shown in the "Municipality Consolidation Draft." I would like you as residents, and each resident, to think about this, and to develop a concept of "creating the future community ourselves." I look forward to the direction this takes, and the Osaka Prefectural Government will not be sparing in its support.

Furthermore, it is also necessary to have perspectives from a broader zone transcending prefectural borders. For example, for the development of the whole zoning area, we need to make best use of whatever accumulation owned by each local government. We can assume that the "full set" policy each prefecture tries to provide, all sorts of facilities must be shifted to the "best mix" policy, under which each prefecture will share and contribute to the work of the whole area. When this happens, I think Osaka must play the leadership role.

I have received the report from the Osaka Prefecture Comprehensive Plan Council about the new comprehensive plan to be a guideline of development of Osaka for the 21st century. With the basic target "Rebuilding Osaka, Invigoration," the report gives a vision and direction for an Osaka where everyone can live happily. This coincides with my vision for the Osaka Prefectural Government administration. From now on, with the result of your discussion at this plenary session, I will make decisions on the administrative plan within the year, taking this into deliberate consideration. I will display the 21st century "Nautical chart" for Osaka and work to make it happen.

CONCLUSION

So far I have talked about the different issues surrounding the Osaka Prefectural Government. I have dared to appeal to the people of Osaka using the words, "Osaka crisis."

There is a possibility that we may see a desperate decline – this is absolutely not a situation to be considered! Things will pick up and be better, somehow.

Eight months have passed since I took office as Governor, hoping that Osaka will shine brightly and have a lasting vitality. I think it is very important that we should free ourselves from this crisis and rebuild Osaka. Although this might seem paradoxical, we should share a "positive sense of crisis" shared by all the people of Osaka. It is only after facing the crisis and uniting in feeling that it should not be like this, I am sure that a strong, forward-moving power will be born. I would like to put together each resident's power into a tremendous concerted energy for Osaka's rebuilding.

I would like all the members of the Osaka Prefectural Assembly and the people of Osaka to give their support and cooperation to the Osaka Prefectural Government administration.

Nina Kurasova

Editor: This portrait of Nina Kurasova came from Dianne Post, an American lawyer with the ABA-CEELI. [American Bar Association-Central and East European Law Initiative]

Nina Kurasova is the head of the Women's Leadership School in Rostov-on-Don and an award-winning journalist focusing on women's rights. Her organization has sponsored seminars on networking, organizing, and lobbying. In November, 1999, they organized, with others, a two-day Public Tribunal on Violence Against Women to address the failure of law enforcement to deal properly with the issue. One of their members came from her hospital bed after a severe beating to testify.

They canvassed the rural areas with a lawyer and a psychologist to find women who would testify on audio or video tape or in person. Over 300 people attended the event which was widely publicized. Afterward, local government criticized the women for bringing disrepute upon the area because "now people will know there is violence here." The women's response is, of course, "let's do something about it."

Other actions have included sitting in on every local legislative session until one communist member told the media it was oppressive to have these women watching their every move. Nina also works with a crisis center to help the victims of violence.

Nina has a wonderfully supportive husband, Vladimir, who was her savior when she fell and broke both hands which for a journalist is a severe disability. She struggled through that and is now back "talking feminist" and getting things done for women. They have one son.

Editor's note: Nina's documentation of violence against women in her area has an echo in Rosario Robles' account of canvassing poor women in the Mexican capital. The women reported that of all the problems they face, "violence in the home" was the worst.

We had a gathering in my county a few years ago to discuss domestic violence, and heard about the practice in San Diego, later adopted in this county, of sending not just a policeman to answer complaints of violence, but a social worker as well. A "team approach" to the problem of domestic violence works better than a strictly police approach. We are learning about the "cycle of violence" that keeps both men and women in unhealthy situations that deeply affect the children in the home.

About "watchdogging" the legislature, I think about the situation in Mongolia when women went to observe the legislature in action. They were limited to 15 minutes of watching, and no records of the deliberations were available to citizens. Clearly, the "oversight" of legislatures is an important citizen function. The word "transparency" has come into use; that government should be <u>visible</u> to the citizens. For this reason, Rosario Robles published her personal financial statement, although not required to do so by Mexican law.

Nina Kurasova

Director, Women's Leadership School
Rostov on Don, Russia

Nina Kurasova

[Written by request for *International Women Speak*]

"WOMEN IN THE RUSSIAN MASS MEDIA"

*R*egardless of what Russian officials, those in power, say, the situation of women in Russia continues to worsen. Unemployment among women and the salary gap between men and women are on the rise. Women are being forced out of structures of power. The results of the recent elections to the highest legislative body, the Duma, provide a fresh example. Against this background, the Russian press makes inequality look normal.

Practically all Russian newspapers, those which have a circulation in millions and those that have a very small circulation and are published in small, local communities, publish materials on feminism on a regular basis. These publications are very negative: the image they portray is frightening: she hates men, she doesn't need a family, she is soulless and calculating.

Since the Soviet era, Russians have become used to trusting the printed word. A certain stereotype of feminism is being imprinted in their consciousness today. The funniest and saddest part is that even among the professional journalists who write about feminism, the majority is not familiar with the ideology of the movement. Several times I bet my male journalist colleagues, "I bet I can tell you several fundamental ideas of feminism, you will agree with it, and you will see that you are one of us." And that is how it turned out to be.

The Russian press has very little to say about women in their life, their problems and their public life. The only topics that have to do with women are beauty contests whether in Moscow or in a remote Siberian village. These publications are accompanied with pictures of half-naked women and contain extended remarks on the glamorous life of top models. What is implied is that beautiful young Russian women should go on the runway and look for a rich spouse ("sugar daddy"). According to these newspapers, the top career for a young woman is to find for herself a rich sponsor (the word used is sponsor). And this word, now widely used, has become ambiguous.

Every day in Russia new "womens magazines" appear and disappear. As a rule, they have female Russian names for titles, "Masha" "Dasha" "Natasha". Glamorous, richly illustrated, these magazines have as their only task to teach a woman how to make her man stay with her, and how to satisfy all his whims and caprices.

The saddest part is that the Russian press is being flooded with scandalous, sensational mateials that feature violence against women. In articles on these topics, the details of violence are savored. They savor the details of violence, but they do not make any moral judgement, do not analyze the causes, do not instill in the reader any disgust with violence.

One of my colleagues who works in an independent, provincial newspaper, once told me that the newspaper editor requires his staff to find factual material about family conflict for each issue. These have to be descriptions of twisted abuse or a murder. "Our readers like that," he says.

Against the background of pervasive violence, including the violence in the Caucasus which is flooding Russia, domestic abuse against women seems insignificant and not serious. And newspapers do all they can to shape a perception in society that violence against women is a norm. We women journalists who have devoted our professional lives to the promotion of women's human rights in Russia face a lot of problems. Regardless of the quality of the material we offer, newspapers are reluctant to publish them. (I am talking about the Russian province where I live.)

"It is too serious and boring," they usually say.

I remember an amusing story. Last year, women's NGO information center "AFINA" that I direct, was holding a seminar on the topic "Techniques of Lobbying the Local Legislature." We invited to the seminar Russian and American experts on lobbying, and we had a serious and substantive discussion about the problems of relationships between the civil society and the legislature. Several members of the local press were also present. The next day, one of the newspapers published a story about the seminar. The title of the article was, "The Feminists of Rostov Support Monica Lewinsky" even though the problem of the President's relationship with Monica Lewinsky, needless to say, was not discussed.

Unfortunately, as long as the Russian press writes about women and quotes women from the "machismo" perspective, Russian society will be apprehensive of changing women's social role in this country. For hundreds of years, the image has been cultivated of a woman sacrificing for sake of a man and his work. This ideal has been instilled in Russian social consciousness as early as the nineteenth century by Russian classical writers, Turgenev, Tolstoy and Dostoevsky.

Can anything change? I want to believe that it can. It can, if first of all we will have a different women's press in Russia; one which will cultivate in women a sense of human dignity, encourage and approve of various possibilities in her life, and support her in her aspirations of self-realization.

Some such women's publications are in preparation, but, unfortunately, they are financed by foreign, philanthropic funds. The Russian State does not need this kind of women's press, perhaps not yet?

Editor's note: to interpret this last sentence, I learned from Dianne Post about the ingrained Russian habit of thinking that change only comes from above, from "the Russian State" and not from pressure for change by citizens and citizen groups.

Queen Noor of Jordan

*H*er Majesty Queen Noor of Jordan was born Lisa Najeeb Halaby on 23 August 1951, to an Arab-American family distinguished for its public service. She attended Princeton University in its first class that accepted women, and graduated in 1974 with a B.A. in Architecture and Urban Planning. She worked on international urban planning and design projects in Australia, Iran, the United States and Jordan, from where she traveled throughout the Arab World to research aviation training facilities. Subsequently, she joined the Royal Jordanian airline as Director of Planning and Design Projects.

Their Majesties King Hussein and Queen Noor were married on 15 June, 1978. They have four children, two sons and two daughters. Since 1978, Queen Noor has played a major role in promoting international exchange and understanding of Middle Eastern politics, Arab-Western relations and current global issues throughout the world. In 1985, the Noor Al Hussein Foundation (NHF) was established to consolidate and integrate the Queen's diverse and expanding development initiatives.

NHF programs successfully advanced and modernized development thinking in Jordan by progressing beyond traditional charity-oriented social welfare practices to integrate social development strategies more closely with national economic priorities. NHF projects promote individual and community self-reliance, grassroots participation in decision-making and equal opportunity with special emphasis on the empowerment of women, and international cooperation. These community projects and efforts in the arts and culture have been recognized by the United Nations and other international organizations as development models for the Middle East and the developing world.

Queen Noor has assumed an advocacy role in the International Campaign to Ban Landmines (ICBL) and is patron of numerous Jordanian and international organizations, including the Landmine Survivors Network, the World Conservation Union (IUCN) and women and peace-building campaigns. She is president of the United World Colleges (UWC), a network of ten equal opportunity international colleges fostering cross-cultural understanding and peace. She is also Honorary Chair of the McGill Middle East Program which brings together Jordanians, Israelis and Palestinians to improve living conditions in the region.

To know more about Queen Noor's projects, visit web site: www.noor.gov.jo.

Queen Noor of Jordan

Jordan

Queen Noor of Jordan

[Address to the Nuclear Age Peace Foundation,
Santa Barbara, California, USA, 6 April 2000]

NAPF Web Site: www.wagingpeace.org

"The Responsibilities of World Citizenship"

Dr. Krieger, Honored Guests, Friends,

*I*t is so much more than an honor for me to be here tonight, to accept your Distinguished Peace Leadership Award on behalf of my husband, His Majesty King Hussein. Of course I must admit to some bias, but as someone who believes in the ideals your organization represents, I cannot think of a more appropriate recipient.

His tireless quest for peace earned him his own people's devotion, and respect the world over. Time and time again, he vividly demonstrated that peace was worth more to him than his own life, from the beginning of his reign, when he braved the same intolerance and hatred which had claimed the life of his grandfather King Abdullah, to the end, when he left his hospital bed to guide the Wye Accord from stalemate to agreement.

When the Middle East seemed forever mired in limbo between peace and war, King Hussein devoted much of his time to promoting an equitable negotiating process that has opened the way, enshallah, ("God willing") to a comprehensive Arab-Israeli peace.

He envisioned a peace that satisfies the aspirations of all peoples of the region, addresses their political, development and security concerns, enhances the region's well-being and secures the interests of the international community; a peace that does not stop with ending the state of war, but that proactively attempts to foster cooperation and prosperity among all neighbors in the region.

As he put it in his address to the Joint Session of the United States Congress in 1994, "We in Jordan have always sought a bold peace. We have been conscious of our responsibilities towards the coming generations, to ensure that they will have the certainty of leading a dignified and fulfilled life. We have sought a peace that can harness their creative energies, to allow them to realize their true potential, and build their future with confidence, devoid of fear and uncertainty."

He realized that peace, although the dream of many in our region, is not instinctive; it is a skill that must be learned. He understood the value of education for peace and democracy and staunchly supported programs which promote cross-cultural understanding and conflict resolution skills. He knew that lasting peace required a new way of looking at the world, a view that transcended borders.

It was these values, an enduring idealism and humanitarian commitment that originally drew together a young activist urban planner and a monarch remarkable for his openness and vision. We shared a dream, in fact many dreams, in spite of the differences in our backgrounds, and working together to pursue them was my practical training in peace-building, throughout our 21 years together.

I am further honored, therefore, to receive your World Citizenship Award, not so much for what it says about me, but for what it says about us. The name of this award should give us pause to think. **More and more every day, by necessity, we are all becoming World Citizens.**

Daily we are witnessing the dissolution of borders; political, economic, and ecological. My husband, among many other things, was a keen pilot, and flying with him taught me the irrelevance of national boundaries. From the air, it is clear that lines on the map are not drawn in the earth. And with modern technical advances, it is possible to communicate instantaneously, independent of any terrestrial borders at all.

Recognizing we are all citizens of the world is the first step towards peace. As you in this audience are particularly aware, being a citizen of the world means realizing that as the world shrinks, there is less and less room on it for weapons and arms, whether in the hands of governments, insurgent groups or individuals.

And, as King Hussein said a quarter century ago: "Nothing is more useless in developing a nation's economy than a gun, and nothing blocks the road to social development more than the financial burden of war. War is the arch enemy of national progress and the modern scourge of civilized men."

As we see all too vividly in our region, where the spending on armaments is the highest per capita in the world, this is a colossal waste of valuable resources: monetary, material and human. The presence and availability of these vast arsenals, rather than acting as a deterrent, actually make it harder to establish a lasting peace. If channeled into human priorities instead, such resources would provide more sustainable forms of social security as a defense against violence.

And it is not just officially sanctioned wars that cause such devastation. In the first half of this century, our wars were mammoth struggles between superpowers and their allies. Now, long-standing ethnic tensions have escaped the restraints of larger state control, and are escalating into conflicts – smaller, more localized, but no less devastating to those caught up in them. The world is becoming both more global and more fragmented, and such conflicts have repercussions far outside their geographical boundaries.

I don't need to tell you that one of the greatest evils, in terms of lost resources and the danger of lost lives, is nuclear weapons. With the end of the Cold War, some people may have felt we could breathe easier, that the danger of nuclear annihilation had receded. But this is no time for complacency about perhaps the greatest single threat that has ever faced humankind.

With the entry of India and Pakistan into the nuclear club, the increased possibility of instability or accident in the Russian military, and the destabilizing influence of clandestine nuclear programs in Israel and Iraq, the dangers are only proliferating. 1.8 tons of explosive power for every person on Earth raises to new heights the definition of overkill.

There has been a great deal of concern in recent years about terrorism and chemical and biological weapons of mass destruction; but what are nuclear arms if not the archetypal weapons of mass destruction? And what is a defense policy based on the threat to murder countless innocent civilians but terrorism on a massive scale?

Nuclear weapons have been declared illegal under international law by the International Court of Justice; they must be considered immoral by anyone with a conscience. **The sheer folly of trying to defend a nation by destroying all life on the planet must be apparent to anyone capable of rational thought. Nuclear capability must be reduced to zero, globally, permanently. There is no other option.**

Less dramatic, but much more of a day-to-day threat in the lives of millions is another type of weapon: "anti-personnel" mines. These pose a more insidious threat to civilians and progress because they continue killing after the conflict has stopped. When peace is declared, the guns and mortars are stilled, but no one turns off the mines.

And because they are small, and destroy lives one by one, their horrific consequences can go as unnoticed as the mines themselves. You may by now be familiar with the ghastly statistics: some 300,000 people around the globe are living with shattered limbs and lives and the number is growing. Every month around 800 people are killed and 1200 maimed by landmines, primarily civilians, often children attracted by their toy-like shapes and colors: a new tragedy every 20 minutes. These indiscriminate killers constitute one of the greatest public health hazards of the late 20th century: a modern man-made epidemic.

As Patron of the Landmine Survivors Network and International Spokesperson for the ICBL, (International Committee to Ban Land Mines) I have visited with survivors in the Middle East, the United States, Vietnam and Cambodia. I have seen first hand the devastation caused by loss of life and limb.

Fortunately, over the last few years, we have witnessed the growth of a new coalition activism, which brought into force, in record time, the Ottawa Landmine Ban Treaty, the first international arms treaty to encompass humanitarian obligations to the weapons' victims. Working together in unprecedented networks, concerned nations, organizations and individuals united in a pledge to win back blighted land, to fulfill our humanitarian responsibilities to the survivors, and to make peace on the ground a reality as well as a declaration.

Inspired by this progress, Jordan hosted in July 1998, the first Middle East Conference on Landmines Injury and Rehabilitation at which I was proud to announce that Jordan was signing the Ottawa Convention which we subsequently ratified. The conference brought together from throughout the Middle East and North Africa the largest group of landmine casualties ever gathered in one place. My country was an unfortunately appropriate place to convene, because the Middle East is littered with, by estimates, more than half of the world's deployed landmines.

In Jordan, children and adults are routinely injured, and about ten percent of our population lives in areas still dangerous and economically unproductive, because of landmines. Scarce agricultural lands and some of the most beautiful and sacred, historic landscapes in the country, especially in the biblical Jordan River Valley, were scarred and forbidden until recently.

Last month His Holiness Pope John Paul II visited Jordan and made a pilgrimage to Bethany, the baptismal site of Jesus Christ. His visit would have been inconceivable only a few short years ago because the area was then heavily mined. There was a sad irony that landmines should hold hostage one of the world's most spiritually significant landscapes, revered by Judaism, Christianity and Islam.

But since 1993, we have cleared the Jordan Valley of some 300,000 mines, to allow those who had tilled the land many years ago, to cultivate it again, and others to unearth once more our region's precious history. Now, pilgrims, who wish to walk in the paths of the prophets, can do so in safety. This ancient and holy ground is no longer desecrated by mines.

The Prophet Mohammed said, "imatatu al-'tha 'an al-tareeq sadaqah": the removal of harmful objects from the path is a good deed." What was once a metaphorical, moral precept is now a literal necessity, a prophecy that has come too true for comfort.

In a few short years the fight to eradicate landmines has gone from a noble dream to international law. But landmines are only the tip of an iceberg in the problem of armaments of every kind, from nuclear weapons to handguns.

Small arms in particular pose a growing threat to conflict prevention and recovery. The indiscriminate sale and distribution of easily carried weapons is the source of a broad spectrum of violence, from schoolyard shootings to civil wars to militia-led genocide, threatening daily the lives of more people than any other menace.

Encouraged first by progress in banning weapons of mass destruction, and then by the unprecedented success of the movement to ban landmines, the Red Cross and other concerned groups have launched similar initiatives against small arms proliferation. Controlling such arms is essential to any lasting peace anywhere in the world; but it is by no means simple. **As Martin Amis put it, "weapons are like money; no one knows the meaning of enough."** What is more, in many cases, weapons are money. The arms trade, both legal and illicit, is a source of tremendous profits, from the military-industrial giants through the gun-runners down to the decommissioned soldier who sells his weapon on the black market.

Ironically, a declaration of peace in one conflict will often lead to an escalation of violence in neighboring countries, as weapons filter from former combatants to informal militias or criminal gangs. Small arms are cheap, easy to obtain, and difficult to trace. They hold a place in the psyche of many cultures that makes them almost impossible to dislodge.

From rural America to Albania to Northern Ireland to Kosovo, the unwillingness to give up guns by those who feel they are their only protection, is one of the greatest threats to peace.

In our rapidly shrinking world, national sovereignty must acknowledge supra-national structures to ensure global safety, just as individuals must recognize the need for balancing their right to defend themselves with the necessity of law to defend everyone.

The progress of the Ottawa Landmines Treaty, which has now been signed by two thirds of the world's governments, is a salutary example. But there are other treaties, the Nonproliferation Treaty for instance, that need more comprehensive support.

And it is important for the United States, in particular, to realize that it cannot expect to be a credible leader amongst the nations of the world if it lags behind in fighting our most serious problems, including mines and nuclear weapons, and if it does not meet its financial obligations, in full, on time and without preconditions, where the United Nations is concerned.

As individuals and as nations, we must move from the law of force to the force of law. It is time for all of us, governments and individuals alike, to embrace, extend and empower the structures for peace created in the past hundred years. We must invest them with the full legal and moral authority to stop violence before it begins.

We must strengthen the mechanisms to resolve disagreements peacefully, and to make their resolution by force unworkable, and ultimately unthinkable, by instilling, in the conscience of every society, a culture of peace.

This fundamental need was the oxygen behind the global effort in 1998 to create a statute for a permanent International Criminal Court, which the Nuclear Age Peace Foundation endorses. Citizens of the world must embrace a culture of peace, moving from armaments to agreements. And so doing necessitates coming to terms with the thorny issue of security. As long as a nation, or a community, or an individual feels threatened, violence and recourse to weapons is never far from the surface. **But like so much else, the definition of security is changing.** Threats to security today come not only from war, but also from economic and social inequities, human rights abuses, marginalization, and poverty. **Over the past decades, my work in Jordan and abroad has been predicated on this premise: that true security is not only a matter of protecting borders from military aggression, but of providing a stable environment for all citizens, women and men, of all races and creeds, to participate fully in commercial and political life.**

Providing the prosperity that underpins peace requires taking advantage of the new techniques and technologies of globalization. In this boundary-less information age, with productivity becoming ever more divorced from physical resources, the uniqueness of each country's contribution is coming to depend more on the distinctness of cultures and the innovation of individuals. For example, the Internet has opened the global market to underprivileged women in Jordan who have been trained by the Noor Al Hussein Foundation to produce handicrafts and industrial garments to sustain themselves and their families.

Their products are globally accessible through the NHF World Wide Web site, which receives e-mail orders from US and other markets. This global connection came at an opportune time as NHF has been turning over the ownership and management of these income-generating projects to the women. Such orders will ensure their long-term sustainability.

The self-esteem and confidence that these women have acquired is as valuable to them as the substantial additional income they earn. In the empowerment of women, especially at the grassroots level, our projects have transformed development thinking in Jordan by moving beyond traditional ineffective social welfare schemes to enable women to become genuine economic and political forces in their communities, thereby increasing their status and influence at every level.

As a result, we have seen significant progress in every aspect of quality of life, from literacy to family income to population control. These women are building stable, healthy and prosperous communities, which in turn can engage in regional partnerships in the wider pursuit of peace. These programs, which combine innovation with respect for local values and traditions, have received international recognition as development models for the Middle East and the developing world. Through a network of regional partnerships, we are supporting their implementation in other countries.

World citizens need to be educated, both in the skills required to participate and prosper in the information economy, and, more importantly, in the skills required for getting along with other citizens of the world. We have seen clearly over the past decades that it is not enough simply to sign a peace treaty. We are very conscious of the importance, if we are to overcome the enmity of previous generations, of encouraging the next generation, the future guardians of peace, to understand both their opportunities in a changing world and their duties towards themselves and others.

Our experience has taught me that education is a supremely effective tool for peace-building, especially when it brings together students of differing ideas, backgrounds, even cultures, at a time in their lives when their minds are most open and receptive to programs emphasizing tolerance, cooperation and conflict resolution. And it can give them the tools to make their voices heard in issues that affect them. I have seen this process at work in a number of institutions, in Jordan and around the world.

For instance, the Jubilee School in Amman serves promising scholarship students from throughout the region, with special emphasis on less developed areas of Jordan, promoting community service, creative thinking, and information technology, leadership and conflict resolution skills. Our graduates excel at the best US and other international universities and are committed to return home to their local communities and make an extraordinary difference.

The problems these future leaders will have to address go beyond politics, economics, or even peace. Being a citizen of the world means realizing that we have a responsibility to the world itself, as well as to its human inhabitants, and to future generations. As King Hussein said to the United Nations Conference on Environment and Development:

"Our goal is to ensure that environmental protection becomes as deeply embedded in our national psyche and in our human spirit as our existing commitments to balanced development, pluralism, human rights, and regional peace based on justice and international law. We are deeply committed to this goal, despite the severe constraints of political, economic and demographic pressures on our country .... for we would be morally, politically, and perhaps even criminally negligent if we were to place financial profits and material comforts above the goal of the integrity of our earth, the welfare of our people, and the life prospects of our children and grandchildren."

I believe that these words best express the responsibilities of a citizen of the world. In accepting this Award, I must once more express my debt to the one I consider the emblematic Citizen of the World: His Majesty King Hussein.

He was a committed member of the global family. His optimistic belief in his fellow man, a deep and abiding humanism, was unshakable. He believed in the power of mediation and reconciliation, and practiced what he believed.

He understood that one can be a citizen of the world, and remain a devoted member of one's own country, culture, and faith. In my own quest to become a world citizen, he was my motivator and my teacher, enabling me to build upon my earliest beliefs about global responsibility and put them to practical use.

In this, he was an inspiration for me, as he clearly was to you, and for countless others around the world, and these Awards, both the one you have conferred upon him, and the one with which you compliment me, are fitting tributes to his work and his ideals.

He would have appreciated them greatly, for they would have been proof, for him, that others shared those ideals. I know he would have been honored and touched if he could have been here this evening. I thank you with all my heart, for both of us.

NOTES

Maude Barlow

Activist, author and policy critic, Maude Barlow is an outspoken crusader for Canadian sovereignty and citizens' rights. She is the Volunteer Chairperson of The Council of Canadians, a non-profit, non-partisan public interest organization supported by more than 100,000 members. As a government watchdog, critic of corporate crime and catalyst for grassroots organizing, The Council works to protect sovereignty and to promote democratic development.

A prominent voice in the great free trade debate of the 1980's, Barlow is credited with leading the fight to defeat the Multilateral Agreement on Investment (MAI). More recently, she has turned her attention to the issue of protecting public ownership and control of fresh water. In addition to leading The Council, she is a director with the International Forum on Globalization (IFG), a worldwide network of individuals and groups working to take democratic control of the global economy.

Barlow is a frequent contributor to newspapers and magazines and is often seen and interviewed on television and radio. She has co-authored a number of books, including the best-selling *Class Warfare: The Assault on Canada's Schools*, with educator Heather-Jane Robertson; *MAI: The Multilateral Agreement on Investment and the Threat to Canadian Sovereignty*, with Tony Clarke, and *Frederick Street: Life and Death on Canada's Love Canal*, with environmentalist Elizabeth May. Her autobiography, *The Fight of My Life: Confessions of an Unrepentant Canadian*, was published in 1998.

Her outstanding contribution to public education has brought awards from the Ontario Teachers Federation and the British Columbia Teachers Federation. She is in demand as a speaker on the shift of power from people and democratically elected governments to transnational corporations and the impact of the shift on our lives. Much of her energy is currently dedicated to strengthening citizens' rights and developing strategies to bring our society and economy under public control while at the same time protecting the environment.

Editor's note: The ardent leadership that created whole nations now can be seen creating a global perspective on the needs of each individual; for water, clean air, peace. Barlow is such a leader; she teaches us to respect every glass of water.

Maude Barlow

Volunteer National Chairperson of the Council of Canadians
Founding Member of the Water Watch Coalition
Canada

Maude Barlow

"THE GLOBAL FRESH WATER CRISIS"

There is a common assumption that the world's fresh water supply is huge and infinite. This assumption is false. Available fresh water represents less than half of 1 percent of the world's total water stock. The rest is sea water, or inaccessible in ice caps, some groundwater and soil. The problem is that while the only renewable source of fresh water is continental rainfall, the world population keeps increasing by roughly 85 million per year. As a result, the availability of fresh water per person is decreasing rapidly. Instead of taking great care with the limited water we have, however, we are diverting, polluting and depleting that finite source of fresh water at an astonishing rate.

Worldwide, the consumption of water is doubling every 20 years, placing enormous pressures on aquatic ecosystems. Today, 31 countries are facing water stress and scarcity. Over a billion people lack adequate access to clean drinking water. By the year 2025, as much as two-thirds of the world's population – predicted to have expanded by an additional 2.6 billion people – will be living in conditions of serious water shortage and one-third will be living in conditions of absolute water scarcity. The United Nations and the World Bank predict that if we do not change our pattern of water waste, by 2025 the demand for fresh water will rise by 56 percent more than is currently available.

Groundwater over-pumping and aquifer depletion are now serious problems in the world's most intensive agricultural areas. Water tables are falling everywhere. Instead of living on water income, we are irreversibly diminishing water capital. At some time in the near future, water bankruptcy will result. Eventually some dry areas will not be able to serve both the needs of farming and those of the cities.

The world's waterways are also struggling with the full range of modern industrial toxic pollution. Over a century of mining, forestry and large-scale industry has affected virtually every water body in Canada and toxic chemicals are found even in the most remote parts of the Far North.

The story is the same all over the world. For example, the Aral Sea basin, shared by Afghanistan, Iran and five countries of the former Soviet Union, was once the world's fourth largest lake. Excessive river diversions have caused the loss of three fourths of its volume while its surrounding wetlands have shrunk by 85 percent. Almost all fish and waterfowl species have been decimated and the fisheries have collapsed entirely. The Aral Sea is one of the planet's greatest environmental tragedies.

There is simply no way to overstate the water crisis of the planet today.

A radical rethinking of our values, priorities and political systems is urgent and still possible. Yet there are forces at work in the world today that, unless challenged, would move the world almost inexorably into a water-scarce future.

THE IMPACT OF GLOBALIZATION

The dominant economic and political system of our time is fuelled by the ideology of economic globalization, the belief that a single global economy with rules set by business and a global consumer market is our inevitable shared future. Economic freedom, not democracy or ecological stewardship, is the defining metaphor of the post-Cold War period for those in power. As a result, the world is going through a transformation as great as any in history. At the heart of this transformation is an all-out assault on every public sphere of life.

Everything is for sale, even those areas of life once considered sacred, such as culture and heritage, genetic codes and seeds and natural resources, including air and water. Increasingly, resources are controlled by a handful of transnational corporations which are now so big, their combined sales surpass the combined economies of most of the world's countries.

A striking feature of economic globalization is the creation of dramatic inequality. This deep inequality is dramatically affecting access of the world's poor to water, the most basic of life's needs. The United Nations says that fully three-quarters of the population living under conditions of water stress are located in developing countries. By 2025, the Commission projects, those low-income countries experiencing water stress will amount to 47 percent of the total world population.

Economic globalization creates economic and political structures that make an ecologically sound economy impossible. To meld their economies with that of the world's, governments are pressed by transnational corporations to implement a set of policies that privatize, deregulate, eliminate trade and investment barriers, boost exports, and generally relinquish state controls over the economy and natural resources. Intrusive technologies, including the massive transportation systems needed to carry out global trade, damage water systems.

THE WATER PRIVATEERS

From water and wastewater services to bottled water for the world's boutique market, the world's most precious resource is seen to hold vast potential for profit. The world of privatized water is overwhelmingly dominated by two French transnationals: Vivendi SA, whose water division is Generale des Eaux, and Suez Lyonnaise des Eaux – the General Motors and Ford Company of the water world. Between them, they own, or have controlling interests in, water companies in approximately 120 countries on five continents and distribute water to almost 100 million people in the world.

In March, 1999, Vivendi purchased U.S. Filter Corp. for over $6 billion in cash, leapfrogging over any rivals in North America and making the merged giant the world's largest water company with an estimated $12-billion in annual sales. Recently, a number of giant pipeline and energy companies have entered the water field, promising great stock profits from what they are calling "convergence" – the prospect of a single company carrying natural gas, water and electricity to millions of customers on a for-profit basis. General Electric has joined forces with the World Bank and investment speculator George Soros to invest billions of dollars in a "Global Power Fund" to privatize energy and water around the world.

United States energy giant Enron, having acquired Wessex Water PLC of Britain, and Phillip's of Canada, is bidding for huge contracts against the established players for newly privatized water services in countries around the world, including Canada. These companies stand to profit from huge windfalls as governments around the world, having allowed their municipal infrastructures to crumble, now hand the wholesale water market over to the private sector. Every year, they meet with leading politicians and World Bank officials at the World Economic Development Congress to promote the privatization of municipal water services.

THE GLOBAL TRADE IN WATER

The water privateers have now set their sights on the mass export of bulk water, by diversion and by supertanker. Turkey's water company is constructing a pipeline that would divert water to the Mediterranean Sea where it would be sold to Cyprus, Malta, Libya, Israel, Greece and Egypt. The Nordic Water Company supplies water from Norway to continental Europe by sea in huge floating plastic bags. To deal with droughts in southern European countries, the European Commission is looking into the possibility of tapping into the sources of water-rich countries like Austria. If its plans to establish a European Water Network are realized, then Alpine water could be flowing within a decade into Spain or Greece rather than into Vienna's reservoirs.

One of the largest proposed diversion projects back on the table for discussion is the GRAND Canal – the Great Recycling and Northern Development Canal which calls for the building of a dike across James Bay at the mouth of Hudson Bay to create a giant freshwater reservoir out of James Bay and the twenty rivers flowing into it. A massive series of dikes, canals, dams, power plants and locks would divert this water down a canal to Georgian Bay, where it would be flushed through the Great Lakes and taken to the United States southwest.

The NAWAPA – the North American Water and Power Alliance – has gone through a similar rebirth. The original plan envisaged building a large number of major dams to trap the Yukon, Peace and Liard rivers into a giant reservoir that would flood one-tenth of British Columbia to create a canal from Alaska to Washington State to supply water through existing canals and pipelines to thirty-five American states.

A Canadian Company, Global Water Corporation, is now engaged in a "strategic alliance to plan an international strategy to move water globally in bulk tankers" with the Signet Companies, an international maritime shipping company based in Houston. The two companies have approached Singapore's Trade Development Board with a proposal to ship Alaskan water to the region; Global says its proposal has been met with favourable reaction. The company bluntly states: "Water has moved from being an endless commodity that may be taken for granted to a rationed necessity that may be taken by force."

The trade in bottled water is one of the fastest-growing (and least regulated) industries in the world. These companies are engaged in a relentless search for new water supplies to feed the global demand. Stories of companies buying up farmland to access its wells and then moving on when supplies are depleted are surfacing in rural communities all over the world. Sometimes, these companies leave dried up systems in a whole area, not just in the private land they bought.

Of course, the global poverty gap is mirrored in the inequitable access to bottled water by the world's people. For the same price as one bottle of this "boutique" consumer item, 3,000 litres of tap water could be delivered to homes. This irony cannot be lost on the industry which peddles its product as environmentally friendly and part of a healthful lifestyle. In fact, however, allowing the world's public water sources to be destroyed while creating a multi-billion dollar industry to provide "pure" water to the world's rich in non-renewable plastic is a form of insanity.

THE FAILURE OF GOVERNMENTS

Governments all over the world have been unforgivably remiss in not recognizing the crisis surrounding the world's water resources and for not planning to take steps to offset the coming emergency. True, in the developed world, there are some real success stories in the reclamation of rivers, lakes and estuaries choked with sewage, and industrial pollution. The partial recovery of the Great Lakes, for example, through joint action of the bordering provinces and states is one. Conservation efforts in Europe and North America have resulted in some reduction in household and industrial water use and helped slow the terrible rate of aquifer withdrawal.

The United Nations declared the 1980s to be the International Drinking Water Supply and Sanitation Decade and made some serious inroads into providing infrastructure and clean water to some particularly desperate communities. But freshwater management is in its infancy and political commitment, public education and conservation awareness are sadly lacking all over the world.

A coordinated effort by the world's governments could change this pattern of wastage within a decade. With current technologies and methods available today, a conservative estimate is that agriculture could cut its water demands by close to 50 per cent, industries by 50 to 90 per cent, and cities by one third with no sacrifice to economic output or quality of life. What is missing is political will and vision.

Through "public-private partnerships," municipal governments in many countries are blurring the lines between private companies and democratically-elected governments. Often, these "partnerships" are the first step to full privatization. And because many of the same companies providing these services also have the ability to move into the area of bulk export, dams and water diversion, governments are granting them access to water resources through the back door.

In fact, governments everywhere appear to be on the privatization bandwagon. The United Nations Economic and Social Council Commission on Sustainable Development actually proposes that governments turn to "large multinational companies" for capital and expert advice, and calls for an "open market" in water rights. At a March, 1998, United Nations conference in Paris, governments proposed to turn water into a global commodity, driven by market forces and called for an enlarged role for the private sector.

The United Nations and the World Bank have formed the World Water Council which brings together governments, the private sector and civil society to address the world's water crisis. The Council works directly with private corporations through its action arm, the Global Water Partnership. The World Bank sponsors a program called "Business Partners for Development" making it clear that some of the biggest private water companies, like Lyonnaise des Eaux, are closely involved and have started to work toward a "Social Charter for Water."

It is clear that transnational water corporations are waging an offensive on many fronts to take over the agenda of international water sustainable development programs for their own profit and governments are allowing it to happen.

Finally, and most important, governments have established very few laws or regulations to protect their water systems. Most haven't even begun to address the issues of privatization, commercialization and trade in water. Some even explicitly grant water rights to the private sector. The most immediate example is the North American Free Trade Agreement (NAFTA) signed by Canada, the United States and Mexico in 1993.

INTERNATIONAL TRADE AND INVESTMENT AGREEMENTS

Chapter 3 of NAFTA establishes obligations regarding the trade in goods. It uses the General Agreement on Tariffs and Trade (GATT) definition of a "good" which clearly lists, "waters, including natural or artificial waters and aerated waters" and adds in an explanatory note that "ordinary natural water of all kinds (other than sea water)" is included. When NAFTA and its predecessor, the Canada-United States Free Trade Agreement, were being negotiated in the late 1980s, Canadian opponents pointed out that water was clearly at risk and asked their government to specifically exempt the trade in water from the agreements.

The Canadian government argued that under Canadian domestic law, NAFTA did not apply because, at the time, no water was being traded for commercial purposes in any of the NAFTA countries. Critics pointed out that this "protection" was temporary; the moment any state or province of any of the three NAFTA countries did allow the sale of water for commercial purposes in the future, water would become a "good" as defined by the GATT, and the provisions of NAFTA would apply.

United States officials confirmed that this was, in fact, the intent of the trade deals when they were negotiated. In 1993, then Trade Representative Mickey Kantor said in a letter to a United States environmental group, "When water is traded as a good, all provisions of the agreement governing trade in goods apply." In other words, the question is moot until one of the governments grants a permit to export water.

Three key provisions of NAFTA place water at risk once it is traded. The first is "National Treatment" whereby no country can "discriminate" in favour of its own private sector in the commercial use of its water resources. Once a permit is granted to export water in one country, the corporations of the other NAFTA partner countries would have the same right of establishment to the commercial use of that country's waters as its domestic companies. If a Canadian company, for instance, gained the right to export Canadian water, American transnationals would have the right to help themselves to as much Canadian water as they wished.

The second provision is "Investor State" (Chapter 11) whereby a corporation of a NAFTA country can sue the government of another NAFTA country for cash compensation if the company is refused its national treatment rights or if that country implements legislation that "expropriates" the company's future profit. Only a "foreign-based" company can sue using Chapter 11; domestic companies have to abide by national law and cannot sue their own government for compensation under NAFTA. There has been a flurry of investor state suits in North America since NAFTA was signed challenging environmental, health and safety legislation in the three countries.

The third provision is "Proportionality" whereby a government of a NAFTA country cannot reduce or restrict the export of a resource to another NAFTA country once the export flow has been established.

NAFTA is not the only existing trade agreement that compromises water. The World Trade Organization (WTO) was created in 1995 at the conclusion of the Uruguay Round of the GATT. Mandated by its 134 members to work toward the elimination of all remaining tariff and non-tariff barriers to the movement of capital and goods across nation-state borders, its central directive is to promote global free trade. The WTO contains no minimum standards to protect labour rights, social programs, the environment, or natural resources.

The WTO includes water; using the same GATT definition of a "good" as does NAFTA. Unlike any other global institution, including NAFTA, the WTO has both the legislative and judicial authority to challenge laws, policies, and programs of member countries if they do not conform to WTO rules, and to strike these rules down if they can be shown to be "trade restrictive." One provision of the WTO particularly places water at risk. Article XI specifically prohibits the use of export controls for any purpose and eliminates quantitative restrictions on imports and exports.

THE NEED FOR COMMON PRINCIPLES

At the start of the new millennium, the world is poised to make crucial, perhaps irrevocable decisions about water. The human race has taken water for granted and massively misjudged the capacity of the earth's water systems. Just as we are beginning to face this reality, forces are already established that would see water become a private commodity to be sold and traded on the open market.

To develop a comprehensive water ethic, we must first acknowledge that there is a profound human inequity in the access to freshwater sources around the world. Those who are water-poor live almost exclusively in the developing world. We have in this situation a tragic dilemma. To "share" the water resources of the developed world, which could be argued is a moral obligation, would put great stress on already stressed ecosystems.

Only water that runs off in rivers to the sea or is mined from aquifers is actually available freshwater. While Canada holds almost one-quarter of the world's freshwater, most of it is in lakes or river systems flowing north. To move large volumes of this water would massively tamper with the country's natural ecosystems.

Scientists warn that removing vast amounts of water from watersheds has the potential to destroy ecosystems. The experience in Canada shows that local climate change, reduced bio-diversity, mercury poisoning, loss of forest, and the destruction of fisheries habitat and wetland have already resulted from existing water diversions and hydro-electric projects.

But what of the humanitarian argument that in a world of water inequality, water-rich areas have an obligation to share water supplies with others? Perhaps here, it would be helpful to distinguish between short-term and long-term situations. For all concerned, importing water is not a desirable long-term solution. Water is such an essential necessity of life, no group should become dependent on foreign supplies that could be cut for political or environmental reasons. By exporting for other peoples' needs, a relationship of dependency would be established that is good for neither side.

As environmental researcher Jamie Linton says, "Perhaps the strongest argument against commercial water export is that it would only perpetuate the basic problem that has caused the 'water crisis' in the first place – the presumption that peoples' growing demands for water can and should always be met by furnishing an increase in the supply. This thinking has led to the draining of lakes, the depletion of aquifers and destruction of aquatic ecosystems around the world."[1]

What I want to propose is a new "water ethic" based on the principle that water is part of the earth's heritage and must be preserved in the public domain for future generations. At stake is the concept of "the commons," the idea that through our public institutions we recognize a shared human and natural heritage. Citizens in their home communities must be the watchdogs of our waterways and must establish community organizations to oversee the wise and conserving use of this precious resource.

We need to agree on a set of guiding principles and values. The following points are offered as an opening dialogue:

1. Water belongs to the earth and to all its species. Modern society has lost its reverence for water's sacred place in the cycle of life and its centrality to the realm of the spirit. Only by redefining our relationship to water can we begin to right the wrongs we have done.

2. Water should be left where it is wherever possible. Nature put water where it belongs. By accepting this principle, we learn the nature of water's limits and how to live within those limits.

3. Water must be conserved for all time. Each generation must ensure that the abundance and quality of water is not diminished as a result of its activities.

4. Polluted water must be reclaimed. The human race has collectively polluted the world's water supply and must collectively take responsibility for reclaiming it.

5. Water is best protected in natural watersheds. The future of a water-secure world is based on the need to live within naturally formed "bioregions," or watersheds.

6. Water is a public trust to be guarded by all levels of government. Water should immediately be exempted from all existing and future international and bilateral trade and investment agreements.

7. An adequate supply of clean water is a basic human right.

8. The best advocates for water are local communities and citizens.

9. The public must participate as an equal partner with government to protect water.

10. Economic globalization will not result in sustainable water supplies.

At the moment, governments are not doing their job to protect our water resources. I believe that a new citizens' movement is going to have to come together to protect the world's water resources and define a new water ethic for the twenty-first century. Within every community and in every country, citizens are going to have to take charge of this issue.

In the long term, nation-states have to establish the regulations and protections necessary to save their water systems. International law must be developed as well that recognizes and enforces the social obligations of global capital in the interests of the global "water commons."

Reference

[1]Quotation from Jamie Linton, *Beneath the Surface, The State of Water in Canada*, Canadian Wildlife Federation. Ottawa, 1997.

Mrs. Maneka Gandhi

*F*ounder and chairperson of People For Animals, Maneka Gandhi has been a vocal advocate of animal rights for her entire political career. She has served on many committees, commissions and governing bodies in her effort to promote the welfare of animals of all species. She has taken a firm stance on animal cruelty as both Chair of the Committee on the Control and Supervision of Experiment on Animals and a patron-for-life member of the Society for the Prevention of Cruelty to Animals.

Born August 26, 1956, Gandhi has gained a worldwide reputation for her remarkable range of activities, both governmental and volunteer. As Chairperson of Rugmark, a non-governmental agency that works to rehabilitate child labor in the carpet industry, she has set up schools and boarding houses for children rescued from the carpet trade.

She was a member of Parliament (Lok Sabha) between 1989 and 1991, and May 1996 onwards, as well as Minister of State for the Ministry of Environment and Forests in two successive governments. Since April 1998 she has held the position of Minister of State for the Ministry of Empowerment and Social Justice.

Her views on animal care are taught in her nine published books, as well as "Surya," a political news monthly she founded and edits. The television programs "Heads and Tails" and "Maneka's Ark" have created awareness on animal welfare all over the country. The only syndicated columnist in India on animal welfare issues, she writes a weekly column published in fifteen national and several international newspapers and magazines. She serves on the boards of several German and British ecological companies. For her work on behalf of animals, Gandhi has been the recipient of more than thirty national awards in India and, in 1992, the premier international award in the field of animal welfare, the Lord Erskine Award of the Royal Society for the Prevention of Cruelty to Animals.

She was married to Shri Sanjay Gandhi, who died on June 23, 1980. She has one son, Feroze Varun Gandhi.

Editor's note: India is blessed by nature with an exceptional abundance of wildlife. The intimate relationship of humans and animals is revealed in the ancient religious texts as well as in the worship of cows today. The stories of Hanuman the monkey and Ganesh the elephant are known by millions of Indian children. The French photographer Ylla produced a book *Animals in India* in the 1950's. She tells of Indira Gandhi's girlhood pet deer and her pandas which she sent to the mountains in the hot months.

Mrs. Maneka Gandhi

Director, People for Animals
India

Mrs. Maneka Gandhi

"Animal Welfare is Human Welfare"

*H*ave you ever thought what your life would be like if you didn't have animals in India?

If there were no dogs and cats in the cities, you would be overrun with rats.

If there were no tigers and other large cats, there would be no forests as the undergrowth would be eaten by herbivorous animals. If there were no forests, there would be no rain and no rivers.

If there were no vultures and crows, there would be rotting carcasses in the fields.

If there were no bullocks, the price of all food would go up because it would have to be transported by truck/train and more fuel would have to be imported.

If there were no cattle, there would be no cooking fuel for the villages and the forests would disappear faster.

If there were no birds and frogs, the volume of pests in the fields would increase uncontrollably and food would become scarce.

If there were no snakes, rodents would eat up even more than the one-third of grain that they consume in the grain silos of the government.

If there were no horses, there would be very little communication between the villges. If camels disappeared, the entire life of the desert would come to a halt.

If there were no monkeys and birds, many forest trees would disappear. As the seeds only germinate after they have been eaten and pass out of their bodies.

If there were no turtles, the rivers and oceans would quickly become polluted and the earth would die.

If there were no earthworms, the soil would deteriorate and become infertile.

If there were no donkeys, there would be no mining, quarrying or construction work.

If there were no butterflies, the plants would disappear.

Each and every species from the bats to the bears, from the hyena to the deer is a protective shield for humans. The quality of our lives depends on them. When we disregard them, kill them, eat them, throw them out of balance by breeding huge numbers of one species for food and killing everything else, smuggle them out for fur and feathers, we are destroying our own small lives.

India is a country where 70 per cent of its people depend on animals – for travel, cooking, transport of all goods and millions of people, for pest control, replenishing the earth's soil and water, for forests and rain, for protecting the land from the oceans, for cleaning the water, for clothing, for food.

And yet, there is NO government budget for their care. There is no government department that looks after their lives. The Animal Welfare Board is given the tiny sum of Rs. 2 crore to look after one hundred million animals, less than 50 paisa per animal. There are no hospitals all over India, no shelters, no ambulances, no veterinary services of any kind. There are no vets trained in wildlife medicine, no bird doctors even though India has 10 per cent of the bird population of the world, no essential medicines to combat epidemics that kill thousands in agony. There is no attempt to stop cruelty, no attempt to make their lives bearable. Our slaughterhouses are the dirtiest and most inhumane in the world, our care of milch animals possibly the worst. We have the largest number of zoos of any country, and yet not a single member of the staff has been trained to look after the imprisoned animals.

We take from these animals all they can give – and more. We give nothing back.

The result is that our own quality of life has deteriorated.

Diseases like salmonella are now rampant. Our waters are polluted, our forests have disappeared, our agricultural land is yielding less and less. As each species disappears, so does the future of our children.

People for Animals attempts to create a new race of Indians who believe in the old traditions of this country. All for one and one for all. Who realise that each human's life is dependant on that of the butterfly and therefore each has its own place and each has to be saved and nurtured.

The purpose of People for Animals is to make a network of brave and dedicated people who will look after animals and stop cruelty wherever they see it. If each one of us takes responsibility for our areas, we can change the world. India has the largest number of laws protecting animals in the world. All we need now is tough, caring people to learn and implement the laws. To make sure that India makes it intact into the next century with all her citizens, animal and human, hopeful for a better life.

You can make that happen. With knowledge, involvement, donations of time, money and expertise. Under the Constitution of India, each animal in this country belongs to each citizen. Which means that you are responsible for the Gangetic Dolphin in Varanasi and the Indian Dog in Kolhapur, the sparrow in Jaipur, and the tiger in the Sunderbans. But most of all, you are responsible for the suffering animal in your city and your street. You can help it. You can form a part of the magic circle of love around it and all other life.

Editor's note:

Gangetic Dolphin, a sea creature found only in the river Ganges.

Varanasi, the new name for Benares.

Sundarbans, the name of a forest.

Sheila Watt-Cloutier

During her five years as president for Canada of the Inuit Circumpolar Conference, Sheila Watt-Cloutier has fought vigorously to rid the arctic region of hundreds of chemical contaminants that pose health hazards to the indigenous Inuit people. She began working on health issues in the mid-1970's when she served as an Inuktitut translator in the Ungava Hospital in the arctic.

Over the next fifteen years, she began turning her energy toward improving health conditions and education in Nunavut, a region of northeastern Canada, where conditions were often sub-standard and dismal. As president for Canada of ICC, she cooperates with Inuit leaders from Russia, Greenland and Alaska, addressing regional health issues. She has made numerous presentations to governments and international bodies such as the Arctic Council and the United Nations environmental agencies.

Predominant among her concerns is the detection and presence of more than two hundred toxic chemicals, including DDT, PCB's, dioxins, mercury, lead, benzene and tuolene which are now found in the breast milk of nursing mothers. A portion of these chemicals, she argues, are transferred to the baby during the first six months of life.

Forced to question the health and safety of the food and wildlife in their region, Watt-Cloutier has led a charge against pollution in the arctic region.

Born in Kuujjuaq, a small Inuit community in northern Quebec province, she and her family were always closely connected to the land they cultivated and the sea around them. She has two adult children and a grandson.

Editor's note: The arctic region is environmentally fragile because it lacks the soil and vegetation cover that absorbs toxic pollution in warmer climates. Dr. Nancy Zak, a native peoples specialist and part Inuit, has attended the bi-annual ICC Conference, and describes the dancing and merry-making, the joking and laughing characteristic of Inuit society. At present, native tribes around the world communicate with each other on the internet, and have begun projects for mutual benefit such as eco-tourism and information sharing.

Sheila Watt-Cloutier

President for Canada of the Inuit Circumpolar Conference
Canada

Sheila Watt-Cloutier

[International POPs Elimination Network Forum Global POPs Process Meeting, Nairobi, Kenya, January 24, 1999]

{Editor's note: POPs means Persistent Organic Pollutants.}

"CHEMICAL POLLUTION IN THE ARCTIC"

Good afternoon. My name is Sheila Watt-Cloutier. I am President for Canada of the Inuit Circumpolar Conference, the organization that defends the rights and interests of Inuit internationally. ICC represents Inuit who live in Alaska, Canada, Greenland and the Chukotka region of Russia. I am delighted to be here today and thank the many people who have made this forum possible, particularly those from International POPs Elimination Network.

I was born in Kuujjuaq, a small Inuit community in northern Quebec. Although most Inuit now live in settled communities and enjoy many of the advantages of modern technology, we remain a people tied to the land. I should, as well, say that we are tied to the sea – for Inuit are also a coastal people.

We are here today to begin the very hard task of negotiating an international contaminants convention beginning with twelve of the deadliest chemicals. Last June, many of us here today met in Montreal to begin this process. I listened to the many different ways these chemicals affect the lives of people around the world. Although our issues may be different, our concerns are the same.

In Montreal, I told you that the levels of many of these substances in the breast milk of Inuit women are higher than anywhere else in the world and of the concerns this information raises amongst our people. Published studies confirm the presence of over 200 chemicals – including DDT, PCB's, dioxin, lead, mercury, toluene, benzene and xylene, not in a hazardous waste site but in mothers' milk. Twenty percent of a mother's total body burden of these fat loving (lipophilic) chemicals are transferred to our babies in the first six months through breast feeding. Exposure to these chemicals has been proven to cause – endocrine effects – that is they damage our reproductive, neurological, and immune systems.

I wonder how we have created a global situation where mothers in the Arctic worry about poisoning their children through their very life giving breast milk, while mothers in other countries rely on these same chemicals to protect their children from disease. This situation is not only immoral but must be deemed intolerable.

Each year more than 6 tons of PCB's fall on Canada's Arctic – my home – from outside Canada. In Montreal, I told you that levels of PCB and other persistent organic pollutants in the "country food" – the wild animals – we eat are so high that we question the health of our wildlife and the safety of our food. In the Arctic, we have few alternatives to the food we hunt – as it is this same food through which we identify ourselves, binding us as family and community, which ultimately sustains us physically and spiritually. We are the land and the land is us. When our land and animals are poisoned, so are we.

When this food source is compromised by contaminants, more than our health is affected: our economy, culture, spiritual well being and way of life are also altered. In the Arctic, the preparation for the hunt and the sharing of the proceeds bind families, communities and generations together. There is nothing in the south to compare with the societal importance of these age-old customs of preparing and sharing to our people.

I have listened with great concern how these same chemicals that are in our Arctic – are harming the environment and are harming the people who use them in many other countries around the world. I am here today not only fighting for the sustainability of the Inuit way of life but for all the people around the world whose voices cannot be heard and who have been and are being harmed by these chemicals. I realize that to solve our problems in the Arctic, we must understand and work together to solve the problems around the world.

We as society have sent people into space and probes to the far reaches of the galaxy, we can perform surgery on the heart of a baby before it is born, we can put computers in the tops of pens – so I find it hard to understand why we cannot find safe alternatives to these deadly chemicals.

Recently in my country, a report was published stating that certain chemicals in children's toys may cause kidney damage. These toys were pulled from the shelves and warnings posted almost immediately. I am proud of the speed at which my government reacted to this important issue, and we now have the information needed to make a choice to buy these products or not. We as Inuit have no choice about our exposure to dioxins, DDT, PCB's and so on. I wonder why so many people have had to suffer around the world while the data and reports and hard science builds up around our ears telling us that these chemicals kill.

I have listened to the many arguments from certain sectors of our society that say these chemicals are safe as long as we manage their risk. I say it is easy for these people to support this regime because they are not an exposed population nor are they the people who are the applicators. I strongly endorse – our host for the coming week – UNEP's Executive Director Klaus Topfer when he said that the ultimate goal of this treaty must be the elimination of POPs production and use and not simply better management, I strongly believe that the eventual Global POPs Convention must be one of elimination rather than risk management.

The Canadian Northern Aboriginal Coordinating Committee on POPs (the NAPCC) is a coalition of the four aboriginal peoples in Canada's north (the Dene Nation, the Metis Nation – Northwest Territories, Yukon First Nations and Inuit). We have prepared a paper which outlines our concerns and our perspective on these negotiations – it is available in the back of the room. In short we must:

- ensure this agreement is one of elimination rather than risk management;
- ensure adequate technology, infrastructure and capacity to establish baseline data for POPs in humans and in wildlife;
- provide appropriate support and financial resources to identify, inventory, and effectively dispose and destroy chemicals in abandoned stockpiles;
- ensure effective export and import prohibitions and monitoring and verification mechanisms to ensure illegal trade in POPs does not occur;
- actively seek safe alternatives to the chemicals that pose an undue risk to humanity;
- provide a well-funded secretariat housed within United Nations Environment Programme, to administer the POPs treaty.

It is our hope that you will support these positions. Through this Convention, we have the opportunity to make our world a little safer for our children and a little more equitable for all people especially those in the developing world. These negotiations toward a global POPs Convention will challenge our capacity to have real vision. They will raise fundamental issues about the relationship between the developed and the developing worlds. Between the rights of commerce and the rights of people.

about the relationship between the developed and the developing worlds. Between the rights of commerce and the rights of people.

These few comments explain why I am here speaking with you today, and why ICC will use its observer status in the UN to press for a **comprehensive, rigorous and verifiable global treaty on POPs.** This is our goal.

I am convinced that to achieve ICC's goal – which I hope many of you share – will take co-operative efforts by all the aboriginal, public health, public interest and environmental communities. We must press, cajole, argue, persuade, communicate, and encourage governments and industry to commit to a global agreement that will protect our health and our environment.

The NAPCC and IPEN have shown us that we are stronger together and that the issues and concerns are ours not theirs and that by working together each one of us can affect real change for a healthier world. To achieve our objective likely requires a global campaign. Certainly Inuit through ICC are prepared to be part of such an international effort.

Thank you.

UNEP: United Nations Environment Programme

IPEN: International POP's Elimination Network

NAPCC: Canadian Northern Aboriginal Coordinating Committee

ICC: Inuit Circumpolar Conference

Marilyn Waring

$\mathcal{D}$r. Marilyn Waring is a farmer, an academic, and a national and international consultant. She is a senior lecturer in social policy and social work at the Albany Campus of Massey University, in Auckland, New Zealand. Dr. Waring received an Honours BA in Political Science and International Politics from Victoria University of Wellington in 1973. In 1989, she was awarded a Doctorate of Philosophy in Political Economy.

At the age of 23, Marilyn Waring was elected to the New Zealand Parliament, an office she held between 1975 and 1984. During that period, she served as Chair of the Public Expenditures Committee, Senior Government Member of the Foreign Affairs Committee, and on the Disarmament and Arms Control Committee. She served three terms before causing a snap election on the issue of the visits of nuclear powered and nuclear armed warships to ports in New Zealand.

Between 1991 and 1994, Dr. Waring was a Senior Lecturer in Public Policy and the Politics of Human Rights with the Department of Politics at the University of Waikato, New Zealand. In 1990, she was awarded the University of Waikato Research Council Grant to continue work on "female human rights." She has worked as a consultant for organizations such as the Food and Agriculture Organization (FAO), the United Nations Development Fund for Women (UNIFEM), the Yukon Territorial Government, the Ford Foundation, and the Ontario Provincial Government.

Marilyn Waring's publications include *If Women Counted*, published in 1988 by Macmillan, *Three Masquerades: Essays on Equality, Work and Human Rights*, published in 1996 by Auckland University Press, *Counting for Nothing: What Men Value and What Women Are Worth*, a reprint of the 1988 book with a new introduction, University of Toronto Press, 1999.

Editor's note: Dr. Waring tells me she has 100 angora goats on her farm, and raises the food for the table in her kitchen garden. She was a chief analyst of the worldwide study of women in parliaments, *Politics: Women's Insights*, conducted and published by the Inter-Parliamentary Union in the Series "Reports and Documents" No. 36. She is the subject of a video that has traveled around the world.

Marilyn Waring

Author, Farmer, National and International Consultant
Associate Professor, Massey University
New Zealand

Marilyn Waring

[Edited extract from *Counting for Nothing* (2nd ed) University of Toronto Press: 1999]

"ACCOUNTING FOR THE LABOR OF WOMEN"

*L*et's deal with my old dilemma: what is the 'cost' of visibility in a patently pathological value system? Do we want all of life to be commodified in an economic model? Must there be only one model, and must economics be at the centre?

We'll begin with consideration of the changes made to the 'boundary of production' in the revision of the rules of the United Nations System of National Accounts[1] (UNSNA) in 1993. Of particular importance is paragraph 1.22, describing the UNSNA as a "multi-purpose system ... designed to meet a wide range of analytical and policy needs". It states that "a balance has to be struck between the desire for the accounts to be as comprehensive as possible" and their being swamped with non-monetary values. The revised system excludes all "production of services for own final consumption within households ... The location of the production boundary ... *is a compromise but a deliberate one that takes account of most users* [my emphasis – it is difficult to make extensive use of statistics in which you are invisible] ... If the production boundary were extended to include production of personal and domestic services by members of households for their own final consumption all persons engaged in such activities would become self-employed, making unemployment virtually impossible by definition".

I would have thought that was a reflection of the inappropriateness of the definition of unemployment, rather than an excuse to leave most of the work done by most women out of the equation. The International Labour Organisation (ILO) specifies that the production of economic goods and services includes all production and processing of primary products, including that for home consumption, with the proviso that such production must be 'an important contribution' to the total consumption of the household.[2]

In a 1993 resolution concerning the international classification of status in employment, the International Conference of Labour Statisticians defined subsistence workers as those 'who hold a self employment' job and in this capacity 'produce goods and services which are predominantly consumed by their own household and constitute an important basis for its livelihood'.[3]

Compare the concepts of 'an important basis for livelihood', and 'an important contribution to the total consumption of the household', with the specific exclusions from production in the 1993 UNSNA. Paragraph 1.25 establishes the "consumption boundary" describing the domestic and personal services which do not count when they are produced and consumed within the same household. These services are the cleaning, decoration and maintenance of the dwelling occupied by the household; cleaning, servicing and repair of household goods; the preparation and serving of meals; the care, training and instruction of children; the care of the sick, infirm or old people; and the transportation of members of the household or their goods. These services do count when supplied by government or voluntary agencies and when they are paid for.

Women all over the planet perform the vast bulk of this work but the authors of the UNSNA call these tasks indicators of welfare, and out of a breathtaking conceptual ignorance and undoubted western bias, fail to grasp there is no demarcation for women in the subsistence household between production inside or outside the consumption boundaries. All tasks of survival in such circumstances are related. The Statistical Commission report: "As far as household production is concerned, the central framework includes for the first time all production of goods in households, whether sold or not, and services *if they are supplied to unity other than their producers*" (my emphasis). As concerned as they have been with conceptual and measurement difficulties, and boundaries of consumption or production, the designers of the new UNSNA just miss the point, and in so doing fail to reflect the reality of the majority of women on the planet.

For example, if a woman spends an hour or more a day fetching water (which in some circumstances, according to the new rules, may be a subsistence activity), she will use it critically and sparingly. She may use it in the care of livestock and poultry, she may use it to assist in food storage or the preparation of food which is marketed or bartered, she may water the vegetables in her garden – all of which may be classified as subsistence activities. She will also use it in food preparation, cooking, cleaning dishes and other utensils. She may wash children and other dependents and clothes. She will probably even recycle the water, so that the same liquid is used first to wash children and then to wash the pig, or first to prepare food for the family and then used to water the garden. Her 'transportation of goods' will also supply the household's drinking water. Half of her work counts; the other half, with the same water, and however critical these activities are as 'an important basis to livelihood', are on the wrong side of 'the deliberate compromise'.

The United Nations Statistical Commission explains that "personal services for own final consumption within the same household are excluded because of measurement and valuation problems".[4] Yet in the same publication the Commission states "the lack of concrete knowledge about the activities of women has been a major impediment to the formulation of policies and programmes, at both the national and international levels, to achieve equality. Revisions of international statistical standards and methodologies may be one tool to overcome these impediments. The 1993 SNA [System of National Accounts] is one of these tools".[5]

The lack of knowledge is admitted as a major impediment for policy making, but because of measurement and valuation problems we still won't recognise the bulk of the work that women do in an unpaid capacity. In some countries it won't matter what the rules say, practices won't even reflect the 1993 changes. I was in Pakistan in 1994, and met with the deputy government statistician in charge of national accounts. He was very aware of the new boundaries, and especially the inclusion of the collection of water, firewood and fodder. In no uncertain terms he told me that he had no intention of counting these activities, as it could then be claimed that most women worked (sic), and as far as he was concerned, they didn't, and that was that.

The trade off is the establishment of satellite accounts, where "extended definitions of the production boundary can be applied where the restrictions of being in line with other statistical systems", (for example, such as on labour market, governmental, financial, or monetary statistics), "are eased in favour of in depth analysis of the real magnitude and economic significance of the production of personal services within the household".[6]

The Statistical Commission probably feels that it has been very responsive to decades of calls for the recognition of such work, culminating in the United Nations Fourth World Conference on Women in Beijing 1995. Paragraph 206(g)(ii) of the Platform for Action called on governments to: "Measure in quantitative terms unremunerated work that is outside national accounts, work to improve methods to assess its value and accurately reflect its value in satellite or other official accounts which are separate from but consistent with core national accounts". Paragraph 212 called for the provision of "resources and technical assistance" in developing countries "so that [these countries] can fully measure the work done by women and men including both remunerated and unremunerated work".

The passage of these paragraphs was supported by the work of the International Women Count Network, coordinated by the International Wages for Housework campaign, which bought the signatures of over 1200 NGO's to call on governments to measure and value the unpaid work of women in satellite accounts of the GDP, and to define the unwaged worker as a worker in the International Labour Office clarifications. The petition stated that "by counting women's work women would count and would be strengthened and their efforts on other issues addressed in the Platform for Action and outside it". Following its passage Ruth Todasco, a member of the International Women Count Network was quoted as saying "only when women's unwaged work is acknowledged and valued will women's demands and needs be valued".[7]

The campaign attracted support globally, and added to calls from the UN Conference on Environment and Development (the Earth Summit in Rio de Janeiro), and the Vienna Declaration following the UN Human Rights Conference. I supported them. Profound policy changes could result from the recognition of this work. But I am increasingly disturbed by the instrument we see as the strategy for delivering this recognition.

'Acknowledgement and valuing' unpaid work for the purposes of policy responses to 'women's demands and needs', does not require the monetary imputation of the value of such work in satellite accounts. Ironically, the statistical surveys necessary to compile the satellite accounts, based on time use, provide what is needed. Yet evidence is already emerging of the 'magnitude and economic significance' of the domestic and personal services excluded from the production boundary of the 1993 UNSNA, but able, you will remember, to be included in satellite accounts.

Economist Duncan Ironmonger had already discovered the magnitude of such production in the Australian economy. He defined the household economy as the system that produces and allocates tradeable goods and services by using the unpaid labour and capital of the household.[8] "The household economy transforms intermediate commodities provided by the market economy into final items of consumption through the use of its own unpaid labour and its own capital goods".[9]

Ironmonger was the first to adapt traditional input – output tables showing the internal structure of the formal business and government sectors of the economy to the household. The traditional measures he called gross market product (GMP). Household input – output tables show the internal activity structure of the informal household sector of the economy, and present the uses of intermediate commodities, labour and capital in each type of productive economic activity undertaken in the households by unpaid labour and own capital. This he labels gross household product (GHP). Gross economic product (GEP) is the total of GMP and GHP.

Using the results of the national time use survey conducted in 1992, Ironmonger found that Australians do about 380 million hours of unpaid household work each week, compared with 272 million hours in paid employment. The value of the unpaid work, calculated at the average salary rate (including fringe benefits) of A$14.25 an hour, was A$283 billion in 1992. Add the contribution from household capital, i.e. $25 billion for equipment and vehicles, and $33 billion for the use of owner – occupied housing, and the GHP was $341 billion, while the GMP was $362 billion. In accounting for more than 48 percent of total production, the household was the single largest sector, exceeding the production of manufacturing by a multiple of ten, and the value of all mining and mineral extraction by a multiple of three.

> If you have been battling for years for the visibility of unpaid work, there is something very satisfying about these findings. The recognition not simply of the 'magnitude and significance' of the household sector, but of its economic paramountcy, gives rise to speculation about its confinement to the satellite accounts. I have always suspected, that far from technical and measurement difficulties being the reason for non inclusion, the fact that this sector was so dominant would invite enormous policy dispute about redistribution and equitable investment. The patriarchs, who profit from the current system, could not and would not countenance this competition. As a result, I have an expectation that satellite accounts will not be main players even in domestic policy making, where international comparability cannot be sustained as argument for remaining with the old framework as the basis of policy making.

Paragraph 206(g)(1) of the UN Beijing Women's Conference Platform for Action called for the conduct of regular time-use surveys to measure unremunerated work, including recording those activities that are performed simultaneously with remunerated or other unremunerated activities. Time Use has figured prominently in the work to establish Genuine Progress Indicators (GPI) in Nova Scotia. Prepared by Dr. Ronald Coleman, the Nova Scotia GPI project has been designated as a pilot by Statistics Canada, which is providing ongoing assistance in data collection and analysis, and staff support.

The indicators include unpaid work, divided into voluntary and community work, unpaid housework and parenting, and the value of unpaid overtime and underemployment. The monetary valuation method used in this study for calculating the economic value of unpaid work is the replacement cost (specialist) method and reflects the hourly wage rate that would be paid in Nova Scotia to replace existing activities at market prices for the same kind of work. While an imputation is used to demonstrate linkages between the market and non market sectors of the economy, a clear focus of the analysis is on time. In 1997 Nova Scotians contributed an estimated 134 million hours of their time to civic and voluntary work, and more than 940 million hours to unpaid household work. Their unpaid work in these two categories was the equivalent of 571,000 full year full time jobs!

Now why are we interested in time. Time is the one thing we all have. We do not all have market labour force activities, we do not all have disposable cash. Many of us do not trade on the basis of money, we trade our time. Our economics is about how we use our time, and even though we frequently do not have a choice about how we choose to use it, it is the common denominator of exchange. Time is the one unit of exchange we all have in equal amounts, the one investment we all have to make, the one resource we cannot reproduce.

On a national level what can time use data tell us? It can show us what goods and services households produce, what the unemployed do with their time, how much additional work children in a household create and whether equality in the distribution of household tasks has been achieved. The use of discretionary time by those in and out of the paid labour force can be analysed. Data may point to inefficiencies in the use of human resources by unnecessary fragmentation of time. It also shows up which sex gets the menial, boring, low status and unpaid invisible work which in turn highlights oppression and subordination.

In rural areas such surveys show seasonal variations, allowing identification of suitable time slots for education and other programmes. Time-use data also provide a measure of the interdependence of the activities of household members, and of how paid work, caring work, housework, community work, leisure, and time spent on personal care are interrelated. This is vital for understanding how the impact of paid labour-force participation of women leads to growth in market activity to replace formerly unpaid activity in the home, or, alternatively, how the devolution of government services of care to the "community" means an increase in unpaid activity by invisible workers.

Time use data also tells when activities are carried out. It assists in planning post-compulsory educational facilities and targeting hours and topics to match current and potential students benefits, libraries, schools, community learning and private educational institutions. The hours when various activities are carried out and for how long provide valuable tools for planners in health services, electricity demand, opening hours of retail outlets, and broadcasting programming. Information on where the population will be and whom they will be with in the event of a disaster like a major earthquake allows informed civil defence planning for different hours and days of the week.

Transport planners need to know about the changing patterns of peoples' activities like hours of work and training, travel times, working from home, and the use of out of school care. Community and voluntary organisation would benefit from knowing how many hours are spent by whom in the broad types of volunteer organisations and how this work is combined with other activities. It may provide useful insights for commercial suppliers on time spent using their types of products or services. It will show how much or how little leisure young people really have, and how they are balancing employment, unpaid work and study. It may well show that the retired population is actually doing a lot of productive work in the community.

In all of these examples it is not necessary to impute monetary values to any person's time use to make policy, to plan, or to monitor and evaluate programmes. The need for the occasional use of imputation is not a reason to abstract all time use data to the economic model. Far more rigorous planning can be achieved by remaining with the time use framework, and it makes much more sense.

Nowhere is the loss of texture and specificity and the policy analysis and consequences more starkly recognised in imputing values of labour than in looking at the consequences to children who work. Stories in the *State of the World's Children 1997* illustrate this. The ILO Minimum Age Convention allows light work at age 12 or 13 but hazardous work not before 18. It also establishes a general minimum age of 15 years, provided 15 is not less than the age of completion of compulsory schooling. Yet we read that of the projected 190 million working children in the 10-14 age group in the developing world, three quarters of them work six days a week or more and one half work nine hours a day or more.[10] In a 1993 study in Malawi, 78 per cent of the 10-14 year olds and 55 per cent of the 7-9 year olds living on tobacco estates were working full or part time.[11] One quarter of the work force, around 50,000, in the glass bangle industry of Firozabad in India, are children under 14 working in indescribably unsafe and inhumane conditions.[12] Haiti has an estimated 25,000 child domestics, 20 per cent of whom are 7-10 years old.[13] In the United States at least 100,000 children are believed to be involved in child prostitution.[14] As many as 3 million children aged 10-14 are estimated to work in Brazil's sisal, tea, sugar cane and tobacco plantations.[15] The most reliable estimates available for the United Kingdom show that between 15-26 per cent of 11 year olds are working.[16]

The answer does not lie in further economic abstractions or colonisation of other disciplines and ways of knowing. It lies with policy making and monitoring and evaluation with approximate accurate input of the interdependencies of the real world, and that does not necessitate a unidimensional economic data base. But if we choose to continue down the perverse and pathological path, and believe that in monetary imputation of all we hold dear we will effect the fundamental paradigm shift the planet needs, then I promise you, we will all be Counting For Nothing.

References

[1]*A System of National Accounts*: (United Nations, New York, 1993).

[2]Fifteenth International Conference of Labour Statisticians: Report II, *Labour Force, Employment Unemployment and Underemployment*, (Geneva, ILO, 1982).

[3]Fifteenth International Conference of Labour Statisticians: Report IV, *Revision of the International Classification of Status in Employment*, (Geneva, ILO, 1993).

[4]United Nations Statistical Commission: *The Reflection of Women's Contribution to Production in the 1993 SNA*, (SNA News and Notes, Issue 2, July 1995), http://www.un.org/Depts/unsd/sna/sna2-en.htm.

[5]Ibid.

[6]Ibid.

[7]*Houston Chronicle*, Friday September 15, 1995.

[8]Duncan S. Ironmonger, 'Modelling the Household Economy', in *Economics, Econometrics and the LINK: Essays in Honour of Lawrence R. Klein*, ed. M. Dutta. North Holland, Elsevier Science Publishers, 1995, 397-98.

[9]Duncan Ironmonger, 'Why Measure and Value Unpaid Work?' *Conference Proceedings on the Measurement and Valuation of Unpaid Work*, Ottawa, Statistics Canada, 28-30 April 1993.

[10]*State of the World's Children* New York, UNICEF, 1997, 25.

[11]Ibid. 38.

[12]Ibid. 37.

[13]Ibid. 30.

[14]Ibid. 26.

[15]Ibid. 38.

[16]Ibid. 20.

NOTES

Ruth Bamela Engo-Tjega

From her origins in West Africa, Ruth Bamela Engo-Tjega has become a global leader on issues of health and community well-being. After earning a doctorate in social sciences from Paris University in 1971, she served as Director of Labour in Cameroon until 1984. She then entered the United Nations administration in the Department of Economic and Social Affairs where she is a senior economic affairs officer. She is featured in the 1995 "A Roll Call of Africa's Distinguished Daughters."

She is a frequent speaker and contributor to regional and global conferences.

In Africa, June, 1998: She represented her office at the summit meeting of the OAU (Organization of African Unity) in Ouagadougou, Burkina Faso – her third summit meeting of the OAU since 1991. In 1997, she helped to develop AIDS prevention strategy at the African-African American summit in Accra, Ghana.

In Asia, October, 1999, in Korea: she organized a workshop on "The Role of African NGO's in Development" at the Seoul International Conference on NGO's. [non-governmental organizations] In 1995, at the Fourth World Conference on Women, in Beijing, China, she organized workshops on "African Food Security" and "Young Women and the Future of Africa."

In Europe: She attended the Founding Congress of the Wittenberg Center for Global Ethics, an initiative of Andrew Young, former United States Ambassador to the United Nations, and Dietrich Gensher, a former German Foreign Affairs Minister. At EXPO 2000 in Hanover, Germany, she presented a paper in a Global Dialogues series on "The Role of the Village in the 21st Century."

Her memberships include the Club of Rome, since 1991, and the International Jury of Futuroscope in Poitiers, France. She is a mother who enjoys writing poetry and collecting memorabilia of traditional African women and African special textiles.

Editor's note: Ruth Engo-Tjega's contemporary story of "Grandmother" who survives the death of her eleven children to AIDS, bearing her loss with courage and faith in the future of the youngest generation, has a remarkable resonance. It brings to mind the strength and character of a fictional woman who survived her loss of children to the medieval plague in Norway in Sigrid Undset's great novel *Kristin Lavransdatter*. The novel, written in the early 1920's must have found echoes in the experience of mothers after the first World War. Undset won the Nobel Prize for Literature in 1928.

Ruth Bamela Engo-Tjega

Founder/President African Action on AIDS
Cameroon

Ruth Bamela Engo-Tjega

[A speech given at Teachers College, Columbia University, New York, at an event called "NO ONE IS ALONE: An Evening to Benefit African AIDS Orphans, June 6, 1999]

"No One Is Alone: Africa Rises Against AIDS"

Dear friends, thank you for choosing to be with us here this evening. There are so many competing activities and shows on a Friday night in New York City that we appreciate your decision to be with us. You surely made a good choice!

Indeed, this evening is different from most, with its multiple facets: it is an evening of entertainment and good food – it is also an evening to measure the impact of HIV/AIDS on the future of Africa, with a particular focus on African AIDS orphans. In so doing, it brings all of us closer together, with the common realization that the sick, the needy, the living and the dying are linked and all are part of our daily lives.

This evening, hopefully, will also help us to think about the kind of society we live in, thought that comes closer to our minds, the closer we come to facing our mortality. Are we part of the whole, or have we evolved into a sort of lonely, insensitive crowd? Is there an alternative, a caring, thoughtful societal model in which we could definitely affirm that no one is alone? Lastly, this evening is a celebration of hope, the kind of hope that leads to unexpected achievements.

During the last 50 years, world-wide, we have witnessed an unprecedented increase in self-centeredness. With the perception that happiness and prosperity could only be measured through material accumulation, people have concentrated on looking after themselves and their immediate families, classes, nations, or race. This behaviour has tended to minimize any involvement with problems beyond ourselves. Sharing with others has become a weakness, almost a mistake which, it was perceived, led directly to poverty. The results of this philosophy are disastrous. As we can all witness today, our global world is poorer, not only in terms of food, clean water, health and sanitation, but poorer in terms of lack of tolerance. The stigma against certain groups, including people infected or affected by AIDS is growing.

But it doesn't need to be that way. As human beings, we are part of an environment which is more than ourselves alone. It includes our fellow human beings, whether they look like us or not, whether they are young or old, whether they are healthy or sick; it includes trees, animals and all the grand facets of nature. It is only when we evolve into this multi-dimensional environment, when we interact with, and are stimulated by other living beings and things, the beauty of our environment, that we grow happier, more creative, socially and mentally balanced. It is only then that we are able to feel the needs of others because we finally understand that our personal survival, security, and happiness are only a very small part of the global picture, and that no one is alone.

The magnitude of the HIV/AIDS epidemic on the African continent has exceeded our grimmest fears. On this day alone, 11,000 African men, women and children have been infected, and 5,500 have been buried. 1997 alone has made 1.7 million AIDS orphans, more than 90% of them in Africa. No part of society is spared – from those with the highest skills and expertise, to the citizens whose labour is essential to the security of communities and States, to rural agricultural workers and others involved in production and economic growth. HIV/AIDS has hit at the nerve centre of our nations with grave consequences, impacting on the very existence of our societies. Yet national AIDS programmes are too often invisible and timid, or collapsing due to inadequate funding and support, resulting in insufficient HIV/AIDS prevention and care services.

In some countries, political leadership has led the population into effective action, and in some communities, individuals and groups have devoted themselves selflessly and with meager resources to providing care and prevention services for people affected and at risk. Clearly, experience shows that positive action has positive impact on the epidemic, and on the lives of people affected.

However, positive interventions are too few, and have not matched the magnitude of the epidemic. There is an urgent need to build on existing efforts and to raise the response to a higher level, giving it greater visibility, greater investment and greater commitment.

Because the media does not always publicize efforts from within the African continent, I would like, here tonight, to signal a few efforts which will help strengthen our own individual commitment:

The Commitment of Phil Lutaya

When Mr. Lutaya, the Ugandan artist and singer who died a few years ago of AIDS discovered from his exile in Sweden that he had AIDS, and when he realized how much his country was devastated by this deadly disease, his fraternity with humankind shifted his attention from a self-centred pity to a universal commitment to life. With an extraordinary inner strength that characterizes heroes, he overcame the weakness of his frail and sick body. Mr. Lutaya then started a difficult journey which took him back to Uganda where he first faced controversy and even insults. But stubbornly, he met people at all levels of Ugandan society, from Government to remote villages, speaking to media, churches, schools, truck drivers, and at the same time singing and dancing. His message became a reality, his call was carried on by those who first opposed him. The day he left Uganda to finally face his death, he was saluted by thousands of candles, eternal lights that will never be extinguished. This heroic action has been extremely well captured in "Born in Africa", a film which features in our programme tonight.

As a result of Mr. Lutaya's pact with universal life, Uganda is today one of the rare African countries with a positive look toward overcoming the AIDS epidemic.

"The Grandmother's Story"

In a recent visit on the continent, I witnessed an unfolding tragedy: the death of the eleventh adult child of a strong African woman. It will be known as the "Grandmother's Story" to protect the family against the stigma. The news of the death of this important man had spread throughout the country. On the date of the funeral, I travelled with my family friends. When we reached the village, we immediately went to the tent where the important man's body lay in state, and joined in the traditional cry and greeting of widows and other close family members. After some time, we were led outside the main tent, to allow new visitors to go through the same process. It took me some time to get out of the main tent because I had yet not greeted the mother of the important man. After leaving the room, I sat nearby, waiting for the next occasion to go back in to greet her. While I was sitting outside, I saw an elderly woman, well dressed and visibly giving instructions on the other side of the compound to a group of women who were actively cooking. I recognized grandmother in this elderly woman and ran to her. As we embraced, I said, Grandma, I worry about you, now that your sole support is gone. Without saying a word, she took my hand and led me under a big tree in the middle of the compound, where a number of graves could be seen. She said: I gave birth to 11 children. I will bury the last one today. She continued saying: I stopped crying the week I had to bury five because of this epidemic. After a few minutes of silence during which I felt completely inadequate, she extended her hand again; but this time, she was showing me a group of young children at play. Then she said: Our ancestors sent me in this world with a clear mission which was to bear and bury 11 children. Today I will start my own mission, which is to ensure that what happened to my children will never happen to my grand children. With that hope and strength we embraced again. I left with my own determination, that my little light will shine as long as I live.

African Action on AIDS was created at the end of 1990 by a group of people who believe with grandmother that those who die should die in peace, fully aware that they are leaving behind the strength of a caring world where no one is alone. It was in the spirit of solidarity with the children like the one grandmother had to raise that African Action on AIDS was created, to promote and support the laudable actions initiated either by individuals or communities in the fight against AIDS and its debilitating effects. Since its inception, AAA has sponsored the education of numerous orphans of AIDS victims, who might have dropped out of school. The first five AAA – sponsored students are enrolled since 1997 in National Teachers' College, the College of Commerce and Makerere University in Uganda. We are proud to announce that since 1992, more that 600 students have successfully completed six years of schooling in Benin, Cameroon, Rwanda, Sierra-Leone, Uganda, Tanzania, Zimbabwe. We have more than surpassed our initial goal of sponsoring the education of 200 teenage orphans by year 2000. During the next academic year 1999-2000, we are committed to sponsoring 650 children.

An important part of AAA activities is AIDS prevention, and activities to keep Africa's youth off the streets. This part of the project is undertaken through the establishment of Centres of Excellence, where young people are trained to know and protect their body, and where they engage in other healthy activities. Each centre has a library, sometimes with computers. These centres are located in Benin, Cameroon, Ethiopia, Ghana, Mali, Tanzania, Sierra-Leone, South-Africa and we intend, with your support, to create more.

AAA has many supporters who give their time, money, computers and mostly love and hope. Some of them are in this room and must be recognized:

*   The organizers of this event: Mariama Djibo, Nana Fosu Randall, George Lamptey, Mariama Darboe Diop, Herta Kaschitz, Nguru Karugu, Rose Arungu Olende, Marie Louise

Roumer, Nene Bah, Mary Toure, Rose Toure, Aziz Ndiaye, Jean Francois Epoko, Eva Forson, Alasebu Gebre Selassie, Alain Handy, Claire Kabore, Paulette Austin, Joyce Buchanan;

*   Particular mention must be made of the Permanent Missions to the United Nations of Cameroon and Gabon who provided beverages and supportive messages;

*   The Baha'i Community, which has since the beginning served as "our mother's kitchen," co-organizing the first AIDS prevention workshop in New York with AAA in 1992, and helped fund part of activities of the centre in Tanzania two years later. Now they are ready to embark on an ambitious video project. Some of their representatives in this room are: Mary Power, Marc & Jenny Field, Bani Gujral;

*   Two of our friends not present here tonight (Louise and Frank Gould) decided to organize the collection and shipment of old computers last December to Ghana, and this year to Cameroon where Frank will also organize a series of computer training workshops during his private visit there;

*   Maureen Satriano is another of our young friends who is in graduate school right here at Columbia University. She is going to write her Summer Semester dissertation on African Action on AIDS as a sustainable tool for AIDS Prevention.

*   The presence of American Express Financial Advisors Inc. among us confirms a trend of social entrepreneurship, as the business community understand that investing in human resources gives benefits to business because it creates a healthy work place and a strong consumer base.

We are grateful for all these forms of commitments. We appreciate the commitment of everyone present here tonight. All of you are important to us. As an unknown author's quotation says "A HUNDRED YEARS FROM NOW, IT WILL NOT MATTER WHAT MY BANK ACCOUNT WAS, THE SORT OF HOUSE I LIVED IN, OR THE KIND OF CAR I DROVE ... BUT THE WORLD MAY BE DIFFERENT BECAUSE I WAS IMPORTANT IN THE LIFE OF A CHILD." While absorbing the wisdom of this quotation, please ask yourself the following question: AM I DOING SOMETHING? Yes, let us give another meaning to that deadly acronym AIDS.

Enjoy your evening and thank you for joining us tonight.

NOTES

Girls and Sport

When a girl wears a tee shirt with just the number 9 on it, her friends know she is a fan of Sun Wen or Mia Hamm, champion sportswomen and team captains seen on television and in advertisements. Nine is the number given to the player in forward position in the very popular game of soccer, played brilliantly by Sun Wen of China and Mia Hamm of the United States.

But nine also stands for Title IX, the United States law of recent times requiring gender equality in public funding of school sports. Since its start in 1992, it has been tested in the courts all the way to the Supreme Court in 1997. It began in a lawsuit brought by NOW, the National Organization of Women. Its language is simple, "No person in the United States shall, on the basis of sex, be excluded from participation in, be denied the benefits of, or be subjected to discrimination under any education program or activity receiving Federal financial assistance."

Girls in college today tell stories of their high school soccer team not being allowed to play on "the boy's playing field" because their games "would wear down the turf." The girls had to raise money to rent a place to play, to buy uniforms, to provide transportation to games with other schools. The school paid for the boy's coaches, uniforms and transportation; girls were expected to cheer from the sidelines. All that is changing, and girls in schools around the world are beginning to enjoy access to the benefits of sport.

Indeed, sport for women is much more than a legal battle, or access to physical training and college scholarships. Sport teaches girls the skills they need: to stay physically healthy, to negotiate points of conflict, to play by agreed rules, to lead a team. Sportsmanship is a democratic ideal that includes respect for the opponent, equanimity in winning or losing, camaraderie, sharing the enjoyment of games, the rule of law, fair play. And when we watch the graceful Olympic divers, the poised gymnasts, the high-energy women soccer players, we recognize how good it is for women to live by the high standards of determination and striving for perfection.

Go, girls!

Sun Wen

Captain, Chinese National Women's Soccer Team
China

Sun Wen

[Editor's note: In China as in most of the world "soccer" and "football" are the same game, but in the United States, "football" means an entirely different sport. For American readers, Sun Wen is a champion "soccer" player.]

"SUNSHINE ON THE GREEN FIELD"

*S*un Wen is the most famous Chinese football player. As captain of the Chinese Women's Football Team, Sun Wen has played in more than 100 matches. With her teammates, she obtained the silver medal at the 1996 Atlanta Olympic Games as well as second place at the 1999 Women's Football World Cup. She also has enjoyed the honor of being named the World's Most Valuable Woman Football Player and Asia's Most Valuable Football Player.

People overseas like to call her Sun. Indeed, Sun Wen is the splendid sunshine on the green football field. With her stamina and combative spirit, accomplished skills, and strong charisma, she has won the admiration of fans all over the world.

Sun Wen once said that the traditional Chinese young woman is gentle, quiet and passive, but she chose to be staunch, optimistic and active, like a rose's thorn in the new age.

Sun Wen has a colorful life off the field. A student with the Chinese Department of Fudan University, she also likes to write poems, sing beautiful English songs and collect dolls.

But different from other young women of her age, most of Sun Wen's daily routine is hard and boring, at the limit of her physical capacity. Often after a day's hard training, she will have to write diaries for the media even though she is often too tired to keep her eyes open.

When asked what she likes to do most, she replies, "To have my hair done, listen to music, watch TV programs and live like any ordinary young woman." But early the next day, she is back on the training ground. She would still like to be the one who trains the hardest.

In 1999, the Adidas Company produced an advertisement with Sun Wen as their spokesperson, which is now known to every household in the country. The setting of the advertisement is the Sun's family home in an ordinary lane in Shanghai many years ago. A father is playing ball with his young daughter. The wide-eyed girl does not like to catch the ball with her hands, but instead hits the ball with her head, breaking a neighbor's window. With another hit to the ball, the small girl changes to a football player wearing the national team's No 4 jersey. Her header finds its way into the net of the opposing team. She is Sun Wen.

In 1982, Shanghai residents had a chance to watch for the first time a live satellite feed of the 12th World Football Cup. The 9 years old Sun Wen was captivated by the black and white ball and the exhilarating atmosphere of the match. From that moment on, she would not walk to school anymore; rather, she would kick every stone she would find along the way as if playing football.

Her father Sun Zonggao, also a football fan, gave Sun Wen a real football when she was 10. And so began the untiring training of football for a small girl and her father, on an open space near their home. When in Grade 6 of primary school, Sun Wen and her team participated in the Nanshi District football match and easily beat all their opponents to win the championship. Throughout the matches her team scored 24 goals, of which 22 were kicked in by Sun Wen.

After such a feat, people in Nanshi District knew there was a little girl who played football very well. The young Sun Wen began to taste the joy of success and became more enthusiastic towards the game.

After graduating from primary school, Sun Wen received two notices of admission, one from the football team of the municipal sports school and the other from Datong High School, a renowned school in Shanghai. People say if one can enter this school, he or she is almost assured of access to university.

But Sun Wen could only choose one of the two. She chose the sports school without any hesitation. Unable to persuade her to attend the famous high school, her parents agreed to let her have a try in the sports school, but made the following agreement with her: first, she could not neglect her cultural studies and had to rank among the first tier in all examinations. Second, she should not be afraid of hardship or fatigue. And third, if she came to see no future in playing football, she must change her direction and enroll in the university.

During her senior year, the girl's football program was suddenly dissolved, keeping only the seven top students to participate in the municipal group training. Sun Wen was not among them. The disappointed Sun Wen accepted her father's advice to give up football and to prepare for the university entrance examination.

Then, in November, as she was walking past the school gate, a teammate caught up with her saying, "Sun Wen, you have been permitted to stay! Go check in, quickly!" This message changed her life and she felt the sky turn to sunshine at once.

In 1990, Sun Wen was chosen for the state team and became a top player at the First Women's Football World Cup held in September 1991 in Guangzhou, thus beginning her successes on the green field.

On July 11th, 1999 at 4:00 AM (Beijing time) over 100 million Chinese fans watched the title match aired live on TV. They cheered and wept for the Chinese National Women's Soccer Team meeting the US team in the finals. Fans were touched by the Chinese players' perseverance in standing alone and cheered for their marvelous skills on the field as well as their calm approach. Among the American, northen European and Chinese teams, Chinese players had no advantage in terms of constitution, but tall and strong bodies were not the only key to the development of women's soccer. It was the unique aesthetics of blending power and grace that absorbed the fans. In physical confrontation, Chinese players contended with other teams with indomitable spirit. It was their intelligence that led them to each victory.

To have spent her youth in such a way, Sun Wen says she does not feel regret because she has shown with her unusual youth that women can realize their football dream. So long as they make the necessary efforts, they can break tradition and paint the most splendid rainbow in their own sky.

Acknowledgments

From the Introduction, lines from the poem, "Now" by Gloria Fuertes, translated by Philip Levine, from *The Other Voice: Twentieth-Century Women's Poetry in Translation*, New York, W. W. Norton & Company, 1976, Bankier, et al.

Talks published by permission.

Photographs:

Mary Robinson, UN/DPI photo by E. Schneider

Louise Frechette, UN/DPI photo by Eskinder Debebe

Angela King, UN/DPI photo by Milton Grant

Najma Heptulla, Photo by Georges Cabrera

Gro Harlem Brundtland, UN photo 178175 E. Debebe

Nafis Sadik, UN photo 183104 by M. Tzovaras

Sadako Ogata, UNHCR/ E. Brissoud, 1991

Queen Noor, photo credit Paul Massey, 1995

Wen Sun, AP/Wide World Photos

Newspaper and magazine sources:

Rosario Robles biography: Julia Preston The New York Times, Feb. 28, 2000

Nafis Sadik biography: Barbara Crossette, The New York Times, Oct. 2, 2000

Sadako Ogata biography: Barbara Crossette, The New York Times, Aug. 12, 2000

Tatiana Dmitrieva and Nina Kurasova biographies, thanks to Dianne Post

"Sun Wen, Sunshine on the Green Field" Information courtesy of Women of China, an English language monthly magazine.

Pamphlets and books:

Dedication page poetry from Wislawa Szymborska, *view with a grain of sand selected poems* New York, Harcourt Brace & Company, 1995

Queen Noor's talk was originally published under the title, "The Responsibilities of World Citizenship," Booklet #41, Waging Peace Series, Nuclear Age Peace Foundation, July 2000. See the NAPF web site at www.wagingpeace.org

Maude Barlow: excerpts; also published as "Private Drain on Public Water" in *Blue Gold the Global Water Crisis and the Commodification of the World's Water Supply*, by Maude

Barlow, A Special Report June 1999, issued by the International Forum on Globalization [IFG] San Francisco, California, USA

Marilyn Waring: excerpts from *Counting for Nothing*, (2nd ed.) University of Toronto Press, 1999 for Canada, the USA and its possessions

DORIS EARNSHAW studied political science at Middlebury College, Vermont, and attended the Middlebury Summer Schools of French and Russian. She received her Ph.D. in comparative literature in 1981 at the University of California, Berkeley. While a graduate student she organized the research and translation of women poets from many languages. She started Alta Vista Press upon retirement from the faculty of the University of California, Davis.

International Women Speak is the third in a series of three "Women Speak" books published by Alta Vista Press: *California Women Speak* (1994) and *American Women Speak* (1995).

Type Styles Used: Dutch 801 Roman

Commercial Script-wp

Fonts found in Word Perfect 9.0

California Women Speak

California's Outstanding Senators,
State Legislators, Mayors and Judges

Barbara Boxer

Dianne Feinstein

Nancy Pelosi

Lucille Roybal-Allard

Maxine Waters

Kathleen Brown

Joyce Kennard

Alice Lytle

Marian Bergeson

Lucy Killea

Diane E. Watson

Delaine Eastin

Sunne Wright McPeak

Sandra Smoley

Susan Golding

Anne Rudin

Introduction by Kate Karpilow
California Elected Women's Association
for Education & Research

Edited by Doris Earnshaw
University of California, Davis

- -

American Women Speak

Words, photographs and biographies of nineteen
outstanding American women

Hillary Rodham Clinton (Keynote Address to the Beijing Women's Conference)

Tipper Gore

Nancy Landon Kassebaum

Dianne Feinstein

Kay Bailey Hutchison

Christine Todd Whitman

Ann Richards

Patricia Schroeder

Corrine Brown

Tillie K. Fowler

Elizabeth Dole

Lynn Martin

Madeleine May Kunin

Jeane J. Kirkpatrick

Hilda L. Solis

Deborah J. Glick

Rosalie E. Wahl

Cheryl A. Lau

Cynthia McKinney

Introduction by Dr. Ruth Mandel
Director, Eagleton Institute of Politics
Rutgers University, New Brunswick, NJ

Editors:
Dr. Doris Earnshaw
María Elena Raymond

Alta Vista Press – Ordering Information

Copy the order form on the following page and mail with a check or money order in US Dollars. If you have an order that requires special attention, call us at 530-756-1684.

Prices per book

California Women Speak	$12.50
American Women Speak	$22.50
International Woman Speak	$22.00
Set of all 3 books	$50.00

Sales Tax

California residents add 7% for Sales Tax

Shipping and Handling

$3.00 per book or $9.00 per set in the U.S. for USPS

$5.00 per book or 15.00 per set in Canada or Mexico for USPS

For Air

$8.00 per book or $24.00 per set international for USPS Air

SPECIAL SHIPPING IS AVAILABLE FOR QUANTITY ORDERS. CALL 530-756-1684.

Cost Calculation Table for U.S. Residents	price per item	shipping & handling	total per item	with CA sales tax
California Women Speak	12.50	3.00	15.50	**16.38**
American Women Speak	22.50	3.00	25.50	**27.08**
International Women Speak	22.00	3.00	25.00	**26.54**
Special: buy all 3 and save $7.00	50.00	9.00	59.00	**62.50**

Cost Calculation Table for Orders from Canada or Mexico	price per item	shipping & handling	total per item
California Women Speak	12.50	5.00	17.50
American Women Speak	22.50	5.00	27.50
International Women Speak	22.00	5.00	27.00
Special: buy all 3 and save $7.00	50.00	15.00	65.00

Cost Calculation Table for Orders from All Other Countries	price per item	shipping & handling	total per item
California Women Speak	12.50	8.00	20.50
American Women Speak	22.50	8.00	30.50
International Women Speak	22.00	8.00	30.00
Special: buy all 3 and save $7.00	50.00	24.00	74.00

Alta Vista Press – Order Form

Name _____

Day Phone_____ Home Phone _____

E-mail _____

Address _____

City _____ State/Province _____

Postal Code _____ Country _____

SHIP TO:

Name _____

Address _____

City _____ State/Province _____

Postal Code _____ Country _____

Day Phone_____ Home Phone _____

E-mail _____

Items	Quantity	Cost per item	Total
California Women Speak	_____	$12.50	_____
American Women Speak	_____	22.50	_____
International Women Speak	_____	22.00	_____
Set of all 3 books	_____	50.00	_____

California residents include Sales Tax – 7% _____

Shipping and handling US Residents: $3.00 per book or $9.00per set _____

Shipping and handling Canada or Mexico: $5.00 per book or $15.00 per set _____

Shipping and handling Other International:

$8.00 per book or $24.00 per set for USPS Air _____

Total enclosed in US Dollars _____

Send with your check or money order to:

ALTA VISTA PRESS   Tel/FAX: 530-756-1684

P.O. BOX 73675   E-mail: avp@dcn.davis.ca.us

DAVIS, CA 95617 USA   web site: http://www.altavistapress.com